hamlyn
QuickCook

hamlyn

QuickCook
Budget Meals

Recipes by Jo McAuley

Every dish, three ways – you choose!
30 minutes | 20 minutes | 10 minutes

An Hachette UK Company
www.hachette.co.uk

First published in Great Britain in 2012 by Hamlyn,
a division of Octopus Publishing Group Ltd
Endeavour House, 189 Shaftesbury Avenue,
London WC2H 8JY
www.octopusbooks.co.uk

ISBN 978-0-600-62392-2

A CIP catalogue record for this book is available from the British Library.

Printed and bound in China.

10 9 8 7 6 5 4 3 2 1

Both metric and imperial measurements are given for the recipes. Use one set of
measures only, not a mixture of both.

Standard level spoon measurements are used in all recipes
1 tablespoon = 15 ml
1 teaspoon = 5 ml

Ovens should be preheated to the specified temperature. If using a fan-assisted oven,
follow the manufacturer's instructions for adjusting the time and temperature. Grills
should also be preheated.

This book includes dishes made with nuts and nut derivatives. It is advisable for
those with known allergic reactions to nuts and nut derivatives and those who may
be potentially vulnerable to these allergies, such as pregnant and nursing mothers,
invalids, the elderly, babies and children, to avoid dishes made with nuts and nut oils.

It is also prudent to check the labels of preprepared ingredients for the possible
inclusion of nut derivatives.

The Department of Health advises that eggs should not be consumed raw. This book
contains some dishes made with raw or lightly cooked eggs. It is prudent for more
vulnerable people, such as pregnant and nursing mothers, invalids, the elderly, babies
and young children, to avoid dishes made with raw or lightly cooked eggs.

Contents

Introduction

30 20 10 – Quick, Quicker, Quickest

This book offers a new and flexible approach to
meal-planning for busy cooks, letting you choose the
recipe option that best fits the time you have available.
Inside you will find 360 dishes that will inspire and
motivate you to get cooking every day of the year.
All the recipes take a maximum of 30 minutes to cook.
Some take as little as 20 minutes and, amazingly, many
take only 10 minutes. With a bit of preparation, you can
easily try out one new recipe from this book each night,
and slowly you will build a wide and exciting portfolio
of recipes to suit your needs.

How Does It Work?

Every recipe in the QuickCook series can be cooked
one of three ways – a 30-minute version, a 20-minute
version or a super-quick and easy 10-minute version.
At the beginning of each chapter you'll find recipes
listed by time. Choose a dish based on how much time
you have and turn to that page.

You'll find the main recipe at the top of the page,
accompanied by a beautiful photograph, as well as
two time-variation recipes below.

If you enjoy the dish, you can go back and cook the other time options. If you liked the 20-minute Mixed Bean Pâté with Pine Nuts but only have 10 minutes to spare, then you'll find a way to cook it using cheat ingredients or clever short cuts.

If you love the ingredients and flavours of the 10-minute Hot and Sour Chicken Salad, why not try something more substantial, like the 20-minute Hot and Sour Chicken Soup, or be inspired to cook a more elaborate version, like Hot and Sour Baked Chicken? Alternatively, browse through all of the 360 delicious recipes, find something that takes your eye – then cook the version that fits your time frame.

For easy inspiration, you can also turn to the recipe ideas on pages 12–19 to get an instant overview by theme, such as Kids' Favourites or Cooking for a Crowd.

QuickCook online

To make life even easier, you can use the special code on each recipe page to email yourself a recipe card for printing, or email a text-only shopping list to your phone. Go to www.hamlynquickcook.com and enter the recipe code at the bottom of each page.

BUD-FISH-GES

QuickCook Budget Meals

This book is full of simple, appealing recipes that prove that you don't have to spend a fortune in order to eat delicious, nutritious home-cooked food. It is perfect for those of us who lead busy lives but still want to provide tasty meals for family and friends, without breaking the bank.

Cooking on a Budget

These simple hints and tips will help your money stretch further at mealtime.

· **Pad it out** It's amazing how much further you can make a meal go by throwing in some cheap carbohydrates or vegetables. For example, turning a lamb curry into a lamb and potato curry, or adding some small pasta shapes or lentils to a soup, can double the number of people it will feed. So pad a dish out, feed your family and freeze the leftovers for another meal.

· **Cook in bulk** Not only is it cheaper to buy and cook in quantity, but it's easier too. Try making up big batches of bolognese, chilli, curry and soups, and then freeze in portions. As well as cutting down on the time spent in the kitchen and the running costs of turning on the cooker every night, this also means that you always have a quick, easy meal to hand. By the time you have ordered your takeaway, you could already be serving a delicious, cheap homemade supper... the ultimate fast food!

· **Don't waste it!** Before you throw things away, try to think if there are other ways you could use them. For example, save bones or vegetable peelings to make stocks, or pop an empty vanilla pod in a jar of sugar to make vanilla sugar.

· **Make your own** So much of what we pay for is preparation and packaging. Buy loose vegetables that haven't been prewashed and trimmed, and meat that hasn't been cubed or cut into strips. Buy big bags of spices and herbs from health-food shops and ethnic food stores. They work out much cheaper and allow you to make your own spice mixes, such as Mexican or Indian, much more cost effectively than buying them ready-made.

· **Experiment!** If you don't have exactly the same ingredients that the recipe calls for, then modify and tailor it to what you do have. Don't rush out to buy one type of pasta shape if you have another in the cupboard. Being on a budget doesn't mean you can't be as creative and inventive as you like!

Think Creatively

There is no denying that supermarkets are convenient, but there are other places to acquire food if you think creatively.

• **Grow your own** Whether you are lucky enough to have the space for a full-size vegetable patch, a small balcony for growing in containers and bags or just a small windowsill for herbs, by growing your own produce you will be doing much more than saving money. You will know where your food has come from; be helping the environment by reducing food miles; feel enormous satisfaction as soon as those first shoots appear; and eating tastier, more nutrient-packed vegetables. Picking your vegetables and herbs just before eating them ensures that they retain as many nutrients and vitamins as possible. Try to get a gardening club going with friends, so that everyone can grow as much as possible and share their gluts of tomatoes, courgettes or beans, saving money for everyone. If you don't have much space but are keen to grow more than just a pot of herbs, look into renting an allotment.

• **Take a trip to the market** Most towns have at least one weekly food market. Try to time your trip as the stallholders are starting to clear away. Whether it's the fishmongers or the fruit and veg stall, there are always items that they want to get rid of, and there are often great bargains to be had on locally grown seasonal produce. You will usually need to cook them on the day, but with proper planning that should not be a problem.

• **Be adventurous** Cooking and eating on a budget doesn't mean having to stick to the same old boring meals day in and day out, or buying from the same discount stores. Look at other places where you might be able to buy cheaply. Buying directly from the farm, for example, can work out cheaper as there are no overheads involved in the transport and selling of the goods. Cutting out the middleman in this way means that the farms will often be able to sell at a more advantageous price to you. This applies not just to fruit and vegetables, but also to eggs and meat. If it means having to buy large quantities, then get together with friends or family and split the purchase between you, saving money for everyone.

· **Don't go shopping!** Well, obviously, you'll still have to go shopping some of the time, but why not try a bit of foraging? A nice long walk in the countryside doesn't just clear the head – it can also fill your basket. Blackberries, mushrooms, nuts, elderflowers and sloes are just a few of the things that can be found growing in our countryside... and all are free. That mushroom risotto or blackberry jam will never have tasted so good!

Hints and Tips for Clever Shopping

With a few clever tricks up your sleeve, a trip to the shops will result in bags full of the most useful and best-value produce on offer, and no unnecessary impulse buys to break the budget.

· **Make a list** Meal planning might sound a bit boring, but writing a list and sticking to it really does save money. Check out any offers beforehand and incorporate them into your weekly planning so that you can use as many reduced-price ingredients as possible. When deciding what you will cook for the week, try to work out what ingredients you will have left over from one meal so that you can use it for the next. This will save money and avoid waste.

· **Never go shopping on an empty stomach** Unless you have willpower of steel, going food shopping with a rumbling tummy is a recipe for disaster! There are just too many easy, tempting and usually expensive items on offer that could quickly blow your budget. Eat before you shop so that you won't be persuaded to purchase unnecessary items for snacking; if you are still tempted, then choose healthier snacks, which will keep you fuller for longer.

· **Beware of cheap meat** Cutting down on the quantity of meat in your diet is a quick way of saving money, but don't cut down on quality. If it's cheap, then it is probably at the expense of the animals' welfare, or because it has been pumped with water prior to being packaged. Try eating it less often and having meat-free days, or opt for the cheaper, lesser-known cuts so that you can still enjoy meat without breaking the bank. For guidance, talk to your butcher, who will be happy to give advice.

· **Buy meat that has had as little preparation done to it as possible** Buying a whole chicken, for example, works out much less expensive than buying two legs, breasts and wings. Not only is it cheaper, but once you have learned how to joint a chicken yourself, you will be left with the carcass for making a great soup or stock.

· **Check out the 'reduced' section of the meat aisle** You may find organic, free-range meat at a fraction of the price because it is approaching its use-by date. Cook it that night, or freeze it on the day of purchase for another occasion.

· **Buy in bulk, cook in bulk** Buying ingredients in bulk may feel more expensive at the time, but you are actually saving money in the long run, as the price per kilo works out lower. If you combine that with buying while products are on offer, you really can make a difference financially. If you buy fresh produce in bulk, then make sure it can be frozen to avoid waste.

· **Buy on offer** All supermarkets these days have good money-saving offers, such as 'buy one, get one free', or products at half-price. If the offers are on things that will actually provide a meal that you can enjoy, make the most of them by purchasing the items while they're on promotion, but do be careful that you don't end up buying luxury items that you don't really need.

· **Substitute** Replace Parma ham with another continental-style cured ham, and Parmesan cheese with another hard Italian cheese; lots of items have cheaper substitutes that are actually perfectly acceptable. Many products are restricted by labelling laws but are often produced in a very similar way to their more expensive counterparts.

Try seeking out cheaper alternatives, such as cooking bacon trimmings instead of rashers, and buying knobbly fruit and vegetables instead of 'perfect' ones – they will still taste the same. Even luxury items such as smoked salmon can be bought for a fraction of the price in the form of smoked-salmon trimmings. The same can be said for meat – ask your butcher if he has any odds and ends that he is willing to part with cheaply.

Substitute supermarket own-brand produce for the better-known, more expensive brands. It works out cheaper, and the quality is often the same.

· **Go abroad** Take a 'trip overseas' by shopping in ethnic stores. Chinese, Indian, Polish, Turkish... the list is endless, and the produce is often much cheaper and fresher. It's possible to

Kids' Favourites

Kids can be hard to please, but these firm favourites will be winners with all the family.

Tandoori Chicken Wings with Raita 56

Aloo Tikki with Coriander and Mint Chutney 94

Tomato and Mascarpone Penne Pasta 98

Homemade Baked Beans 116

Grilled Macaroni Cheese with Bacon 140

Deconstructed Shepherd's Pie 154

Minced Pork Balls with Sweet and Sour Sauce 164

Tuna Rissoles with Coriander Mayonnaise 184

Lemon Grilled Fish with Cheesy Mashed Potato 212

Crunchy Baked Apples and Pears 238

Old-Fashioned Rock Cakes 252

Almost Instant Peach Trifle 276

Cooking for a Crowd

When there are lots of mouths to feed, practicality and value for money are the keys to success.

Mixed Bean Pâté with Pine Nuts 30

Meze Plate 42

Lemon and Spinach Soup with White Rice 60

Creamy Mushroom and Tarragon Rigatoni 76

Sweet Potato and Coconut Rice 82

Bulgar Wheat with Goats' Cheese and Red Onion 84

Lentil Bolognese 114

Chunky Vegetable and Cheese Gratin 118

Chorizo and Butter Bean Salad 134

Creamy Cider Chicken with Rice 152

Spiced Shortbread Squares with Toffee Ice Cream 254

Ginger and Lemon Cupcakes 266

Winter Warmers

These comforting dishes are designed to warm heart, soul and body.

Tomato and Chickpea Stew 26

Creamy Wild Mushroom Soup 36

Ham and Pea Soup with Crispy Bacon 48

Giant Tomato and Rosemary Muffins 52

Gardener's Pie 80

Mustardy Squash, Carrot and Sweet Potato Casserole 92

Beef Pies with Crunchy Topping 148

Herby Sausages with Potato and Celeriac Mash 150

Baked Aubergine with Lamb and Pine Nuts 178

Melting Chocolate Pots 248

Sticky Toffee Apples 250

Pear and Walnut Muffins 264

Summer Specials

Welcome the summer with some hot flavours and sizzling salads, perfect for lazy meals alfresco.

Roasted Chickpeas with Spinach 68

Ginger and Coriander Turkey Burgers 128

Cajun-Spiced Hot Dogs 156

Double Whammy Beef Burgers with Pickles 158

Turkey Milanese with Aioli and Garlic Bread 162

Prawn, Avocado and Coriander Tostada 186

Teriyaki Salmon Sticks with Bean Sprout Salad 196

Blackened Sardines with Yogurt Dressing 206

Creamy Mustard and Trout Pasta Salad 208

Spiced Mackerel and Couscous Salad 220

Lemon Tart with Vanilla Cream 262

Raspberry Ripple Pain Perdu 274

Impress Your Guests

Elegant meals don't have to break the bank, nor do they have to take hours to prepare.

Hot and Sour Chicken Salad 38

Creamy Baked Eggs with Blue Cheese 58

Pork Schnitzel with Feta and Butter Bean Salad 130

Fried Steak with Green Peppercorn Sauce 142

Baked Chicken with Lime 144

Pan-Fried Gnocchi and Chorizo Salad 170

Thai-Flavoured Mussels with Coconut Milk 198

Chilli Crab and Rice Cakes with Lime Dipping Sauce 210

Garlic Breaded Salmon with Spring Onion Mash 228

Chocolate and Nut Fondue 234

Sweet Almond Frittata 240

Quick Cherry Tiramisu 258

Ten-Minute Wonders

When you're running out of time or energy, these easy options will feed the family with minimal fuss.

Quick Quesadillas 24

Cauliflower Coleslaw
Pockets 62

Courgette and Garlic
Chilli Fusilli 78

Feta, Spring Onion and
Walnut Tartlets 96

Brie and Thyme Melts 100

Warm Tomato, Liver and
Bacon Salad 146

Chilli and Anchovy
Dressed Pasta 200

Smoked Trout and
Rice Noodle Salad 214

Lemony Tuna and
Borlotti Bean Salad 222

Strawberry Yogurt Crunch 242

Banoffee Pancakes 246

Almond Affogato 272

Midweek Suppers

These comforting dishes are a pleasure to cook and eat after a busy day.

**Warm Mushrooms
with Potato Rosti** 28

Patatas Bravas 40

Chicken Noodle Broth 50

**Chorizo and Red Pepper
Tortilla** 54

**Baked Peppers with Feta
and Spring Onion** 104

**Vegetable Noodles with
Stir-Fry Sauce** 120

**Pork, Mushroom and
Lemon Tagliatelle** 136

**Sesame Chicken
and Noodles** 172

Ham and Mushroom Risotto 174

**Simple Sausage, Bean and
Vegetable Stew** 176

**Frying-Pan Pizza
with Anchovies** 194

**Spaghetti with Broccoli,
Lemon and Prawns** 216

Hearty Fillers

These hearty dishes are filling and satisfying and won't disappoint a healthy appetite.

All Day Breakfast Wrap 34

Chilli con Verduda 88

Spicy Kidney Beans with Rice 110

Farmhouse Meatballs with Couscous 126

Keema Matar with Mango Chutney 132

Golden Pork Chops with Parsnip and Apple Mash 160

Easy Fish Pie with Crunchy Potato Topping 190

Golden Pollack with Homemade Chips and Herby Peas 204

Crunchy-Topped Cod and Leek Pasta Bake 226

Creamy Vanilla Rice Pudding 244

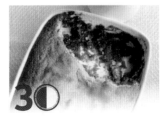

Ginger and Treacle Sponge 256

Fallen Fruit Crumble 270

QuickCook
Soups and
Snacks

Recipes listed by cooking time

30

20

10

 Quick Quesadillas

Serves 4

200 g (7 oz) refried beans
8 soft flour tortillas
25 g (1 oz) jalapeño pepper slices,
  drained and chopped
1 large tomato, deseeded
  and diced
150 g (5 oz) Cheddar cheese,
  grated
2 spring onions, sliced
1 tablespoon finely chopped fresh
  coriander (optional)
100 ml (3½ fl oz) soured cream,
  to serve (optional)

- Spread the refried beans over 4 of the tortillas. Top with the jalapeño slices, diced tomato, Cheddar, spring onions and chopped coriander, if using. Cover each one with another tortilla to make 4 quesadillas.

- Toast the quesadillas, one at a time, in a large ridged griddle pan over a medium-high heat for 30–60 seconds on each side, until lightly browned and the cheese inside has melted.

- Cut the quesadillas into quarters and serve immediately with soured cream, if using.

2 Quesadilla-Style Pizzas Warm the refried beans and spread half over 4 large tortillas. Top each with a second tortilla, then spread the remaining beans on top. Place on 2 large baking sheets, and top with the jalapeño slices, the diced tomato, sliced spring onion and 400 g (13 oz) canned kidney beans that have been drained, rinsed and warmed through. Scatter over the cheese and cook in a preheated oven, 200°C (400°F), Gas Mark 6, for 10–12 minutes until the cheese is melted and bubbling. Cut into slices and serve hot with soured cream, chopped coriander (if using) and shredded iceberg lettuce.

3 Spicy Bean Burritos Spread the refried beans over all 8 tortillas, then top with the jalapeño slices, 2 large, diced tomatoes, 1 chopped red pepper and the sliced spring onion. Tuck in the ends and roll each tortilla tightly, then place in a snug-fitting ovenproof dish. Pour a 300 g (10 oz) jar hot Mexican salsa over the tortillas, then dot with small spoonfuls of soured cream and sprinkle with the cheese. Cook in a preheated oven, 220°C (425°F), Gas Mark 7, for 20–25 minutes until hot and bubbling. Serve hot with shredded iceberg lettuce and chopped coriander, if using.

20 Tomato and Chickpea Stew

Serves 4

2½ tablespoons olive oil
1 large onion, chopped
1 green pepper, chopped
1 garlic clove, chopped
2.5-cm (1-inch) piece of
  fresh root ginger, peeled
  and chopped
1 teaspoon ground cumin
1 teaspoon ground coriander
2 tablespoons tomato purée
500 ml (17 fl oz) hot vegetable
  stock
4 large tomatoes, each cut into
  8 wedges
2 x 400 g (13 oz) cans chickpeas,
  drained and rinsed
salt and pepper
2 tablespoons chopped flat leaf
  parsley, to garnish

- Heat the oil in a large, heavy-based saucepan or casserole. Add the onion, pepper, garlic and ginger, and cook for 6–7 minutes, until softened.

- Stir in the ground spices and cook for a further minute. Add the tomato purée, vegetable stock, tomato wedges and chickpeas, then cover and bring to the boil. Season generously, reduce the heat and simmer for about 8 minutes, until thickened slightly and the tomatoes have softened.

- Ladle into 4 warmed bowls and serve garnished with the chopped parsley.

10 Tomato, Chickpea and Spinach Salad

Cook 3 thinly sliced spring onions, 1 chopped red pepper and the garlic and ginger, following the main recipe, adding the ground spices for the final minute. Dice the tomatoes and place in a large bowl with the chickpeas, 4 handfuls of baby spinach leaves and the parsley. Season to taste and add the cooked vegetables. Toss well together, divide between 4 shallow bowls and serve immediately.

30 Tomato and Chickpea Soup

Cook the onion, pepper, garlic and ginger as above. Add the vegetable stock, tomato wedges, 1 x 400 g (13 oz) can chickpeas, drained, and 500 g (1 lb) passata. Season generously and simmer gently for 15 minutes. Use a hand-held blender to blend the mixture until smooth. Ladle into 4 warmed bowls and serve with a spoonful of natural yogurt and the chopped parsley to garnish.

Warm Mushrooms with Potato Rosti

Serves 4

3 potatoes, scrubbed but
  unpeeled, about 625 g/1¼ lb
  total weight
½ onion, very thinly sliced
4 tablespoons vegetable oil
50 g (2 oz) butter
1 garlic clove, chopped
250 g (8 oz) button mushrooms,
  thinly sliced
2 tablespoons finely chopped
  parsley (optional)
salt and pepper
1 large bunch of watercress,
  to serve

- Cook the potatoes whole in a large saucepan of lightly salted boiling water for 8–10 minutes. Drain and set aside to cool slightly. Wearing rubber gloves to protect your hands from the heat, coarsely grate the potatoes and mix in a bowl with the sliced onion, 2 tablespoons of the oil and plenty of salt and pepper.

- Heat the remaining oil in a large nonstick frying pan and add the rosti mixture, pushing down to flatten it so that it covers the base of the pan. Cook for 7–8 minutes, then slide on to an oiled plate or board. Flip the rosti back into the pan to cook the other side for 7–8 minutes until crisp and golden.

- Meanwhile, melt the butter in a frying pan and cook the garlic and mushrooms gently for 6–7 minutes, until softened and golden. Season to taste with salt and pepper, then stir in the chopped parsley, if using.

- Cut the rosti into wedges, then arrange on serving plates, scatter over the watercress and spoon over the warm mushrooms with their juices. Serve immediately.

1 **Garlic Mushrooms on Toast** Melt the butter and fry the garlic and mushrooms, following the main recipe. Heat a ridged griddle pan and toast 4 large slices of sourdough or rustic-style bread until crisp and nicely charred. Top with the watercress and spoon over the hot garlic mushrooms. Serve immediately.

2 **Warm Mushroom, Potato and Watercress Salad** Cook 750 g (1½ lb) new potatoes in a large saucepan of lightly salted boiling water for 12–15 minutes, until tender. Meanwhile, heat 2 tablespoons oil in a large frying pan and cook the sliced onion gently with the garlic for 7–8 minutes, until softened and golden. Stir in the mushrooms and cook for a further 3–4 minutes, until tender. Drain the potatoes really well, then add to the frying pan with the chopped parsley and toss in the buttery juices for 1–2 minutes to coat. Toss with the watercress and serve immediately.

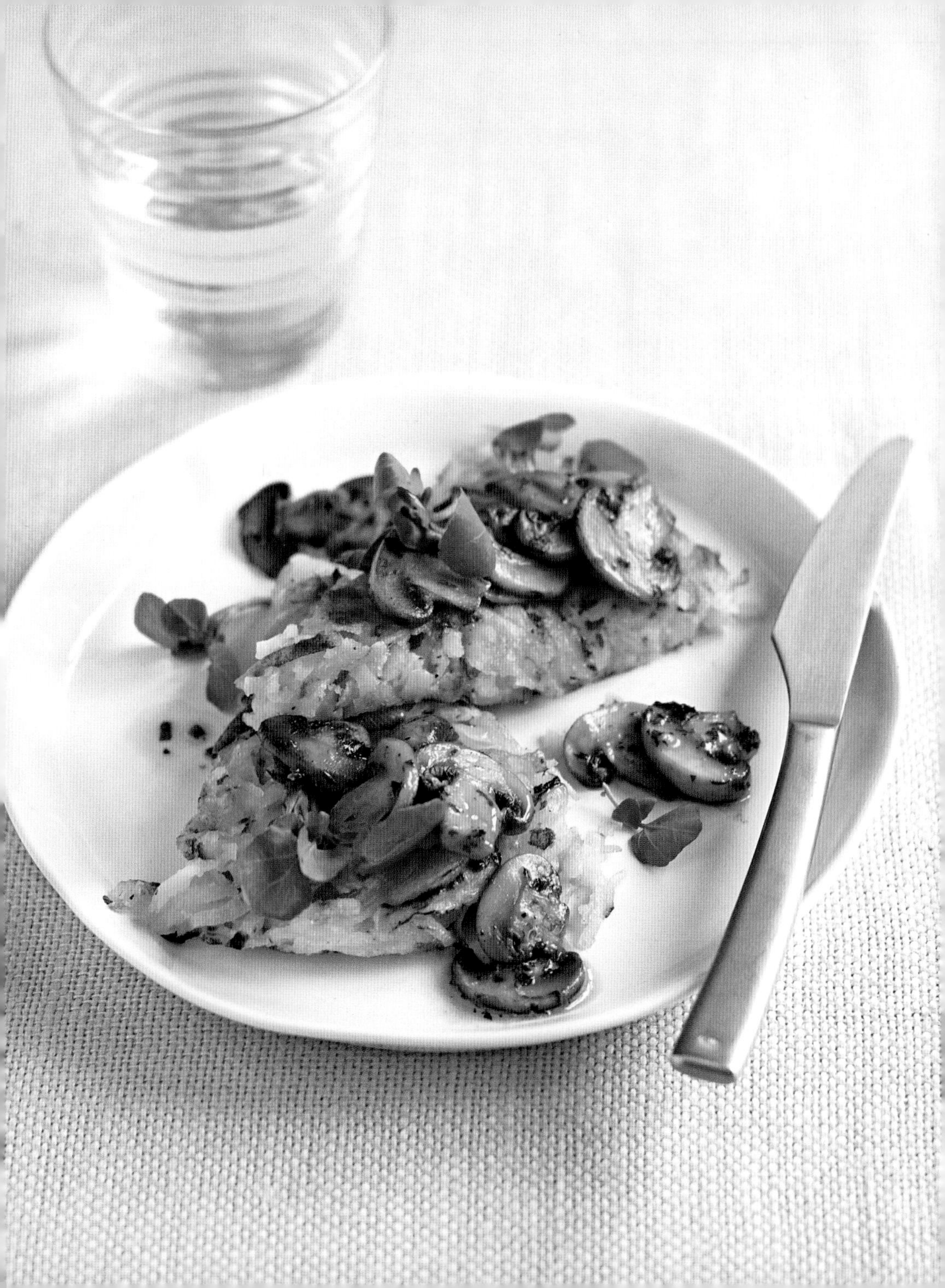

Mixed Bean Pâté with Pine Nuts

Serves 4

2 tablespoons olive oil
1 large red onion, chopped
1 garlic clove, chopped
½ teaspoon hot smoked paprika
2 tablespoons pine nuts
400 g (13 oz) can mixed beans in
  water, drained
1 teaspoon lemon juice
2 tablespoons chopped chives
3–4 tablespoons natural yogurt
salt and pepper

- Heat the oil in a nonstick frying pan and cook the onions for 5 minutes, then add the garlic and cook for a further 3 minutes, until soft and golden. Add the smoked paprika for the final 30 seconds, then remove from the heat.

- Meanwhile, toast the pine nuts in a small, dry frying pan for 2–3 minutes, until lightly golden, shaking the pan frequently to prevent burning.

- Tip the beans into a food processor with the lemon juice, half the chives and the onion mixture. Season well, then pulse briefly, adding enough yogurt to make a rough-textured pâté.

- Spread the pâté on to hot toast and scatter with the toasted pine nuts and remaining chives. Serve immediately with celery sticks.

Quick Bean Pâté Place the beans in the food processor with 4 tablespoons cream cheese with chives, ½ teaspoon dried onion powder and a pinch of dried garlic powder. Pulse briefly to create a rough-textured pâté, then season to taste and spread on hot toast. Sprinkle with the smoked paprika, toasted pine nuts and 1 tablespoon fresh chives, if desired.

Roasted Mixed Bean Salad Cut the red onion in half and slice into thin wedges. Toss with the beans, garlic, paprika, 3 tablespoons olive oil and seasoning. Tip into a roasting tin and cook in a preheated oven, 200°C (400°F), Gas Mark 6, for 20–25 minutes until golden. Meanwhile, toast the pine nuts following the main recipe. Mix 150 ml (¼ pint) natural yogurt with the chives and lemon juice, and season well. Remove the beans from the oven, leave to cool for 5 minutes, then toss with 125 g (4 oz) rocket leaves. Divide between 4 shallow dishes, scatter with the pine nuts and serve immediately with the yogurt dressing.

BUD-SOUP-LAE

 # Swiss Cheese Melts

Serves 4

1 large French stick

200 g (7 oz) Swiss cheese, such
as Emmental or Gruyère, grated

1 tablespoon wholegrain mustard

2 tablespoons mayonnaise

2 tomatoes, deseeded and
chopped

pinch of black pepper

1 round lettuce, to serve
(optional)

- Cut the French stick in half, then slice each half horizontally to form 4 long pieces.

- Place the grated cheese in a bowl with the remaining ingredients and mix well to combine.

- Spoon the topping over the cut side of each piece of bread and place on a baking sheet. Cook under a preheated hot grill for 3–4 minutes, until golden and bubbling. Serve hot with lettuce leaves, if desired.

---

2 **Swiss Cheese Pasta Sauce**

Slice 1 large onion and fry gently in 2 tablespoons vegetable oil for 6–7 minutes, until soft and golden. Stir in 1 tablespoon wholegrain mustard, 2 tomatoes, deseeded and chopped, 275 ml (9 fl oz) double cream and 200 g (7 oz) grated Swiss cheese. Season well with salt and pepper, then stir over a gentle heat until the cheese has melted. Serve over cooked pasta, accompanied by a crusty French stick.

3 **Swiss Cheese and Tomato Tart** Roll out 500 g (1 lb) puff pastry to form a rectangle, approximately 20 x 30 cm (8 x 12 inches). Mix together 1 tablespoon wholegrain mustard and 2 tablespoons mayonnaise, and spread thinly over the pastry base, leaving a 1.5-cm (¾-inch) border. Slice 3 tomatoes thinly and arrange over the mustard mix. Scatter with 200 g (7 oz) grated Swiss cheese, then sprinkle with 1 teaspoon dried mixed herbs. Bake in a preheated oven, 200°C (400°C), Gas Mark 6, for about 20 minutes, until the pastry is crisp and golden. Serve in slices with the lettuce.

All Day Breakfast Wrap

Serves 4

1 tablespoon vegetable oil,
  plus extra for greasing
375 g (12 oz) pork sausagemeat
250 g (8 oz) mushrooms, sliced
2 large eggs
2 tomatoes, deseeded and diced
4 large soft flour tortillas
salt and pepper
brown sauce, barbecue sauce
  or tomato ketchup, to serve
  (optional)

· Preheat the oven to 200°C (400°F), Gas Mark 6, and lightly grease a baking sheet. Divide the sausagemeat into 4 long, flat sausages. Place on the baking sheet and cook in the preheated oven for 15–18 minutes, turning once, until cooked through.

· Meanwhile, heat the oil in a frying pan and cook the mushrooms for 4–5 minutes, until softened and golden. Transfer to a bowl and keep warm. Place the frying pan back over a medium heat.

· Crack the eggs into a bowl and beat lightly. Stir in the chopped tomato, season with salt and pepper and pour into the hot frying pan. Stir gently until it starts to set, then cook for 1–2 minutes, until the base is golden and the omelette is just set. Slide on to a chopping board and slice thickly.

· Place 1 baked sausage in the centre of each tortilla, then top with some mushrooms and strips of omelette. Roll tightly and cut in half diagonally. Serve hot with brown sauce, barbecue sauce or tomato ketchup, if desired.

All Day Breakfast Eggy Bread Halve 2 tomatoes, drizzle with oil and place cut side up on a foil-lined grill rack with 8 bacon rashers. Cook under a preheated grill for 8–10 minutes, turning the rashers once, until the bacon is crisp and the tomatoes are slightly softened. Meanwhile, beat 4 eggs with 3 tablespoons milk and season. Dip 4 slices of bread in the egg mixture. Heat 2 tablespoons oil in a frying pan and add the bread. Cook for 7–8 minutes, turning once, until golden. Serve immediately with the grilled bacon and tomatoes.

All Day Breakfast Tortilla Place 8 thin pork sausages on a foil-lined grill rack and cook under a preheated grill for 10–12 minutes, turning occasionally, until cooked through. Meanwhile, heat the oil in a large frying pan and cook 150 g (5 oz) chopped bacon for 5–6 minutes, until golden. Add the sliced mushrooms and cook for a further 4–5 minutes. Beat 5 eggs lightly and season with black pepper. Add to the pan and stir occasionally until it begins to set. Slice the tomatoes thickly, then remove the sausages from the grill and carefully slice in half lengthways. Arrange the sausages and tomatoes over the tortilla, and cook under a moderate grill for a further 3–4 minutes, until set and golden. Serve cut in wedges with hot, buttered toast.

 # Creamy Wild Mushroom Soup

Serves 4

15 g (½ oz) dried wild mushrooms
125 ml (4 fl oz) boiling water
25 g (1 oz) butter
2 tablespoons olive oil
4 shallots or 1 onion, chopped
1 trimmed celery stick, sliced
1 potato, about 200 g (7 oz),
  peeled and diced
1 large garlic clove, finely chopped
500 g (1 lb) mushrooms, roughly
  chopped
750 ml (1¼ pints) hot vegetable
  stock
2–3 tablespoons single cream
salt and pepper
1 tablespoon chopped chives,
  to garnish
crusty bread, to serve (optional)

- Place the dried mushrooms in a bowl with the measured boiling water, then cover and set aside to soak.

- Heat the butter and olive oil in a large saucepan or casserole. Add the shallots, celery, potato and garlic, and cook gently for about 10 minutes, until softened.

- Squeeze the excess moisture from the soaked mushrooms and chop finely, reserving the soaking liquid. Add both soaked and fresh mushrooms to the pan and cook for a further 4–5 minutes, until softened.

- Strain the reserved soaking liquid into the pan along with the vegetable stock, and simmer gently for 8–10 minutes. Remove the pan from the heat and use a hand-held blender to blend until smooth. Season to taste with salt and pepper, then stir in the cream. Ladle into 4 deep bowls. Garnish with chopped chives, sprinkle with extra black pepper and serve with crusty bread, if desired.

Creamy Mushroom Ciabatta Melt 25 g (1 oz) butter in a frying pan. Cut 500 g (1 lb) mushrooms in half, add to the pan and cook for 5–6 minutes, until soft and golden. Stir in 150 ml (¼ pint) single cream, plenty of salt and pepper and 1 tablespoon chopped parsley or chives, and cook for a further minute. Toast 4 chunky slices of ciabatta or rustic-style bread on a griddle pan and top with the mushroom mixture. Serve immediately.

 Creamy Wild Mushroom Stroganoff Place 15 g (½ oz) dried wild mushrooms, 4 shallots and 1 large garlic clove in a mini-chopper, and blend until very finely chopped. Cook in a frying pan with 25 g (1 oz) butter and 2 tablespoons olive oil for 4–5 minutes, until softened. Add 300 g (10 oz) thickly sliced mushrooms and cook for a further 2–3 minutes. Then add 125 ml (4 fl oz) dry white wine and 250 ml (8 fl oz) double cream, and simmer gently for 6–7 minutes. Stir in 2 tablespoons lemon juice, 1 tablespoon chopped parsley, a pinch of grated nutmeg and plenty of salt and pepper. Serve with brown basmati rice.

Hot and Sour Chicken Salad

Serves 4

250 g (8 oz) cooked chicken,
  roughly chopped
150 g (5 oz) salad leaves
125 g (4 oz) button mushrooms,
  thinly sliced
1 red chilli, deseeded and finely
  chopped
1 small bunch of coriander, leaves
  stripped and chopped
1 tablespoon tom yum paste or
  Thai red curry paste
4 tablespoons vegetable oil
2 tablespoons lime juice
2 tablespoons roughly chopped,
  roasted, salted cashew nuts
  (optional)

- Toss the chicken in a large bowl with the salad leaves, mushrooms, chopped chilli and coriander, then divide between 4 plates.

- Place the tom yum paste, vegetable oil and lime juice in a jar with a tight-fitting lid, and shake until thoroughly combined. Drizzle over the salad, scatter over the cashew nuts, if using, and serve immediately.

20 Hot and Sour Chicken Soup

Heat 450 ml (¾ pint) chicken stock or water in a large saucepan with 6 tablespoons tom yum paste, and bring to the boil. Add 250 g (8 oz) sliced raw chicken breast, then reduce the heat and simmer for 7–8 minutes, until the chicken is cooked. Stir in 200 ml (7 fl oz) coconut milk and 125 g (4 oz) button mushrooms, thinly sliced, and simmer for a further 1–2 minutes, until the mushrooms are just tender. Ladle into deep bowls, then squeeze over the lime juice and serve garnished with the chopped coriander leaves and chilli, if desired.

30 Hot and Sour Baked Chicken

Cut 3–4 slashes into each of 4 chicken breasts and rub all over with 3 tablespoons tom yum or Thai red curry paste. Finely chop the stalks from a small bunch of coriander and mix with 500 g (1 lb) sliced mushrooms. Scatter over the base of a large, foil-lined roasting tin and top with the chicken breasts. Drizzle over 200 ml (7 fl oz) coconut milk, then cover tightly with a large sheet of foil. Cook in a preheated oven, 220°C (425°F), Gas Mark 7, for 20–25 minutes until cooked through. Squeeze over the lime juice and serve with 500 g (1 lb) rice, steamed and garnished with the chopped coriander leaves and chilli, if desired.

30 Patatas Bravas

Serves 4

750 g (1½ lb) waxy potatoes, peeled and cut into bite-sized pieces

5 tablespoons olive or vegetable oil

1 large onion, sliced

2 garlic cloves, crushed

½ teaspoon cayenne pepper or hot chilli powder

½ teaspoon hot smoked paprika

500 g (1 lb) passata

2 tablespoons sherry vinegar

pinch of sugar

salt and pepper

2 tablespoons chopped parsley, to garnish (optional)

- Cook the potatoes in a large saucepan of lightly salted boiling water for 10 minutes, until just tender.

- Meanwhile, make the tomato sauce. Heat 2 tablespoons of the oil in a deep frying pan and cook the onion for 4–5 minutes, then add the garlic and cook for a further 2–3 minutes, until softened. Add the cayenne pepper and paprika, and cook for 1 minute, then pour in the passata, sherry vinegar, sugar and plenty of salt and pepper. Bring to the boil, then reduce the heat and simmer gently for 15–20 minutes, until thickened, adding a splash of water if the sauce becomes too dry.

- Drain the potatoes thoroughly. Heat the remaining oil in a large nonstick frying pan. Fry the potatoes over a medium heat for 15–20 minutes, turning occasionally, until crisp and golden, then stir in the tomato sauce, ensuring the potatoes are coated thoroughly.

- Divide the patatas bravas between 4 shallow bowls. Sprinkle with the chopped parsley, if using, and serve immediately.

 Patatas Gnocchi Bravas Heat the oil in a large frying pan and pan-fry 500 g (1 lb) fresh gnocchi for 4–5 minutes, until crisp and golden. Meanwhile, chop 4 large tomatoes, place in a bowl with ½ teaspoon hot smoked paprika and 2 tablespoons sherry vinegar, and season. Remove the gnocchi with a slotted spoon and keep warm. Tip the tomatoes into the hot pan and stir for 2–3 minutes, until they begin to soften. Spoon into shallow bowls, top with the gnocchi and serve immediately.

Healthy Patatas Bravas Heat 2 teaspoons oil in a deep frying pan and cook 2 garlic cloves, chopped, for 1–2 minutes, until softened. Add ½ teaspoon cayenne pepper or hot chilli powder and ½ teaspoon hot smoked paprika, and cook for a further 30–60 seconds, then stir in 500 g (1 lb) passata, 2 tablespoons sherry vinegar and a pinch of sugar, and simmer gently for 15–18 minutes, until thickened. Meanwhile, cook 750 g (1½ lb) small new potatoes in a saucepan of lightly salted boiling water for 12–15 minutes, until tender. Serve the potatoes with the spicy tomato sauce.

Meze Plate

Serves 4

butter, for greasing
1 egg
1 tablespoon milk
375 g (12 oz) pre-rolled puff
  pastry, about 30 x 20 cm
  (12 x 8 inches)
3 tablespoons grated
  Parmesan-style cheese
200 g (7 oz) feta cheese
5 tablespoons olive oil
1 teaspoon dried oregano
400 g (13 oz) can chickpeas,
  drained and rinsed
2 tablespoons lemon juice
1 teaspoon ground cumin
1 garlic clove, crushed
3–4 tablespoons natural yogurt
salt and pepper
75 g (3 oz) mixed olives

- Preheat the oven to 200°C (400°F), Gas Mark 6, and lightly grease a baking sheet. Beat the egg in a small bowl with the milk. Place the puff pastry sheet on a clean surface and brush with the beaten egg mixture. Sprinkle over the grated cheese, then fold the pastry in half lengthways and press lightly. Cut into 1-cm (½-inch) strips and twist slightly. Place on the prepared baking sheet and cook in the preheated oven for 12–15 minutes, until crisp and golden.

- Meanwhile, cut the feta into thick slices and arrange on a plate. Drizzle with 1 tablespoon of the olive oil and sprinkle over the oregano and a pinch of black pepper. Set aside.

- Place all but 2 tablespoons of the chickpeas in a food processor with 3 tablespoons of the olive oil, the lemon juice, cumin and garlic, and pulse to combine. Add enough yogurt to blend to a smooth but thick paste, then season to taste and scrape into a bowl. Scatter over the reserved chickpeas and drizzle with the remaining olive oil.

- Remove the cheesy puff pastries from the oven and serve with the sliced feta, homemade hummus and a bowl of mixed olives.

---

10 Meze-Style Nibbles
Heat a griddle pan until hot and toast 8 small flour tortillas for 30–60 seconds, turning once, until crisp and lightly charred. Cut into wedges and serve with 200 g (7 oz) sliced feta cheese, 75 g (3 oz) mixed olives and 200 g (7 oz) each of ready-made hummus and taramasalata.

30 Meze-Style Tart
Cut a pre-rolled 375 g (12 oz) puff pastry sheet into quarters to make 4 rectangles, approximately 15 x 10 cm (6 x 4 inches), and place on a lightly greased baking sheet. Scatter over 25 g (1 oz) baby spinach leaves, leaving a border of about 1 cm (½ inch), then fold up the border to make raised edges. Toss 200 g (7 oz) drained chickpeas in a bowl with 1 crushed garlic clove, 1 teaspoon ground cumin and 1 tablespoon olive oil, then season lightly and scatter over the spinach. Crumble 100 g (3½ oz) feta cheese over the top and brush the pastry edges with a little beaten egg. Cook in a preheated oven, 180°C (350°F), Gas Mark 4, for about 20 minutes until crisp and golden. Serve with 75 g (3 oz) mixed olives.

BUD-SOUP-LOU

Stilton, Potato and Leek Soup

Serves 4

50 g (2 oz) butter
2 leeks, chopped
2 garlic cloves, finely chopped
750 g (1½ lb) floury potatoes, peeled and diced
1.5 litres (2½ pints) hot vegetable or chicken stock
100 g (3½ oz) strong Stilton or other blue cheese, crumbled
100 ml (3½ fl oz) single cream
salt and pepper
1 tablespoon chopped chives, to garnish

- Melt the butter in a large, heavy-based saucepan or casserole, and cook the leeks and garlic gently for 5 minutes, until soft and lightly golden. Add the potatoes and cook for a further 1–2 minutes, then pour in the hot stock.

- Bring to the boil, then reduce the heat and simmer for 15–20 minutes, until the potatoes are really tender. Use a hand-held blender to blend until smooth.

- Add the Stilton and cream, and stir until melted, then season to taste and ladle into 4 deep bowls. Sprinkle with the chives and serve immediately with crusty bread.

---

1 **Stilton and Potato Bake** Pour 275 ml (9 fl oz) single cream into a saucepan with 2 finely chopped garlic cloves, 100 g (3½ oz) strong Stilton or other blue cheese, crumbled, 1 tablespoon chopped chives, 2 sliced spring onions and plenty of black pepper. Cook over a medium heat for 1–2 minutes, until the cheese has melted. Meanwhile, arrange 12 ready-made potato cakes or farls in a large, shallow ovenproof dish, overlapping slightly. Pour over the hot cream mixture and cook under a preheated grill for 6–7 minutes, until golden and bubbling. Serve with crusty bread and green salad leaves.

2 **Stilton and Gnocchi Bake** Melt 50 g (2 oz) butter in a large, heavy-based saucepan or casserole, and cook 2 chopped leeks and 2 finely chopped garlic cloves gently for 5 minutes, until soft and lightly golden, then pour in 275 ml (9 fl oz) single cream, 1 tablespoon chopped chives and plenty of black pepper. Meanwhile, cook 500 g (1 lb) ready-made gnocchi in a large saucepan of lightly salted boiling water according to packet instructions, then drain and tip into a shallow ovenproof dish. Pour over the hot leek and cream mixture, crumble 150 g (5 oz) Stilton over the top and place in a preheated oven,

230°C (450°F), Gas Mark 8, for 12–15 minutes until golden and bubbling.

Buttery Prawns on Toast

Serves 4

4 slices of granary bread or
  seeded bread
100 g (3½ oz) butter
pinch of cayenne pepper
300 g (10 oz) raw prawns, peeled
1 tablespoon lemon juice
2 tablespoons chopped chives
salt and pepper

- Toast the bread until golden and crisp.

- Place a large frying pan over a medium heat and melt the butter with the cayenne pepper. Once the butter begins to froth slightly, add the prawns and cook for 2–3 minutes, stirring occasionally, until they are pink and cooked through.

- Add the lemon juice, then stir in the chives and season to taste. Spoon the prawns and their buttery juices on to the hot toast and serve immediately.

Buttery Prawn Spaghetti Cook 400 g (13 oz) spaghetti in a large saucepan of lightly salted boiling water for 11 minutes, or according to packet instructions, until al dente. Meanwhile, cook 300 g (10 oz) raw peeled prawns in 100 g (3½ oz) butter and a pinch of cayenne pepper, as above. Stir in 1 tablespoon lemon juice and 2 tablespoons chopped chives, then season. Drain the pasta, return to the pan and add the prawns and their juices. Stir to combine, then add 75 g (3 oz) rocket leaves and toss briefly before heaping into 4 shallow bowls. Serve with lemon wedges and cracked black pepper.

Buttery Baked Prawns with Rice Melt 50 g (2 oz) butter with 2 tablespoons olive or vegetable oil in a large, deep-sided ovenproof frying pan. Add 1 very finely chopped onion and cook for 5 minutes, until lightly golden. Stir in 2 finely chopped garlic cloves and ½ teaspoon each of ground nutmeg and cayenne pepper. Cook for a further minute, then add 200 g (7 oz) basmati or long-grain rice and stir for 1 minute. Stir in 450 ml (¾ pint) hot vegetable or fish stock, then season generously and cover with a lid. Place in a preheated oven, 200°C (400°F), Gas Mark 6, for about 15 minutes, until the rice is tender and the liquid has been absorbed. Scatter 300 g (10 oz) raw, peeled prawns and 2 tablespoons chopped chives over the rice, then drizzle over 1 tablespoon lemon juice and 2 tablespoons melted butter. Cover and return to the oven for a further 3–5 minutes, until the prawns are just cooked. Spoon into 4 bowls and serve with lemon wedges, if desired.

Ham and Pea Soup with Crispy Bacon

Serves 4

2 tablespoons olive or
  vegetable oil
1 large onion, chopped
1 large potato, about 250 g
  (8 oz), peeled and diced
2 garlic cloves, chopped
300 g (10 oz) frozen peas
1 litre (1¾ pints) hot ham or
  vegetable stock
300 g (10 oz) piece of cooked
  ham, chopped
8 slices thin streaky bacon,
  rind removed
freshly ground black pepper
crusty white bread, to serve

- Heat the oil in a large, heavy-based saucepan or casserole, and add the onion, potato and garlic. Cook gently for 6–7 minutes, until softened.

- Add the peas, stock and ham, and season generously with black pepper. Bring to the boil, then reduce the heat and simmer gently for about 10 minutes, until the potato is tender.

- Meanwhile, place the bacon rashers on a foil-lined grill pan and cook under a preheated grill for 5–6 minutes, turning occasionally, until crispy and golden. Chop or crumble the grilled bacon into small pieces. Drain on kitchen paper.

- Use a hand-held blender to blend the soup until smooth and ladle into 4 bowls. Top with the crispy bacon and serve immediately, accompanied by crusty white bread.

Pea and Lentil Soup Drain a 400 g (13 oz) can green lentils in water and place in a medium saucepan with 300 g (10 oz) frozen peas, 300 g (10 oz) cooked ham, chopped, and 1 litre (1¾ pints) hot ham or vegetable stock. Bring to the boil, season with black pepper and simmer gently for 5–6 minutes. Meanwhile, cook 8 thin streaky bacon rashers, rind removed, following the main recipe. Blend the soup until smooth, ladle into 4 bowls and serve topped with the crispy bacon.

Pea and Ham Risotto Melt 25 g (1 oz) butter with 1 tablespoon olive oil, and cook 1 large chopped onion and 2 chopped garlic cloves for 6–7 minutes, until softened. Add 350 g (11½ oz) risotto rice and stir for 1–2 minutes, until the grains are translucent. Stir in 200 ml (7 fl oz) dry white wine and cook until it has been absorbed, then add 1 litre (1¾ pints) boiling ham or vegetable stock, a small ladleful at a time, stirring frequently until all the liquid has been absorbed and the rice is just tender. This should take 17–18 minutes. About 2 minutes before the end of the cooking time, stir 300 g (10 oz) frozen peas and 300 g (10 oz) chopped ham into the risotto. Meanwhile, grill 8 thin streaky bacon rashers, rind removed, following the main recipe. Serve the risotto spooned into bowls, topped with the crispy bacon.

 # Chicken Noodle Broth

Serves 4

- 4 skinless chicken thighs, about 350 g (11½ oz) total weight
- 1.2 litres (2 pints) chicken or vegetable stock
- 2 tablespoons vegetable oil
- 1 red pepper, cored, deseeded and sliced
- 4 spring onions, cut into 1.5-cm (¾-inch) lengths
- 1 tablespoon chopped fresh root ginger
- 200 g (7 oz) button mushrooms, sliced
- 250 g (8 oz) medium dried egg noodles
- 1–2 tablespoons dark soy sauce
- 2 tablespoons chopped fresh coriander

- Place the chicken thighs in a saucepan and pour over the stock. Bring to the boil, reduce the heat and simmer gently for about 20 minutes, until the chicken is cooked through.

- Meanwhile, heat the oil in a large saucepan or wok, add the red pepper and spring onions, and cook for 4–5 minutes. Add the ginger and mushrooms, and cook gently for a further 4–5 minutes, until softened and golden.

- Use a slotted spoon to remove the chicken thighs from the stock and set aside to cool slightly. Add the noodles to the stock, turn off the heat, cover and set aside for 4–5 minutes, until just tender. Add the cooked vegetables and season to taste with the soy sauce.

- Once the chicken thighs are cool enough to handle, remove and discard the bones, then shred the meat and return to the soup. Ladle the soup and noodles into 4 large bowls. Scatter with the chopped coriander and serve immediately.

 Chicken Noodle Salad Cook 250 g (8 oz) medium dried egg noodles according to packet instructions. Cool under cold running water. Meanwhile, slice 1 red pepper, 4 spring onions and 200 g (7 oz) button mushrooms. Combine 4 tablespoons vegetable oil, 2 teaspoons sesame oil (if using), 2 tablespoons light soy sauce and 2 teaspoons minced ginger (from a jar). Toss the cooled noodles with the vegetables and dressing, and serve immediately, scattered with 2 tablespoons chopped fresh coriander, if desired.

 Chicken, Noodle and Broccoli Broth Thinly slice 4 skinless, boneless chicken thighs. Heat 2 tablespoons vegetable oil in a large saucepan or wok, add 4 spring onions, cut into 1.5-cm (¾-inch) lengths, and 125 g (4 oz) small broccoli florets, and cook for 4–5 minutes. Add the sliced chicken and 1 tablespoon chopped fresh root ginger, and cook for 4–5 minutes, until the chicken is cooked and golden. Add 1.2 litres (2 pints) chicken or vegetable stock, bring to the boil and season to taste with 1–2 tablespoons dark soy sauce. Cook 250 g (8 oz) straight-to-wok rice noodles according to packet instructions, and divide between 4 deep, warmed bowls. Ladle the soup on top and scatter with chopped coriander, if desired.

Giant Tomato and Rosemary Muffins

Serves 4

3 tablespoons groundnut oil, plus extra for greasing
2 tablespoons grated Parmesan-style cheese
200 g (7 oz) plain wholemeal flour
1 teaspoon baking powder
¾ teaspoon bicarbonate of soda
¼ teaspoon black pepper
1 teaspoon dried rosemary
½ teaspoon ground onion powder
¼ teaspoon ground garlic powder
50 g (2 oz) sun-dried tomatoes, chopped
275 ml (9 fl oz) full-fat natural yogurt
2 large eggs, beaten
2 tablespoons sun-dried tomato paste or tomato purée

- Preheat the oven to 200°C (400°F), Gas Mark 6, and grease a 6-cup giant muffin tin or Yorkshire pudding tin, with holes approximately 9 cm (3½ inches) across and 5 cm (2 inches) deep.

- Mix half of the cheese in a large bowl with the flour, baking powder, bicarbonate of soda, black pepper, rosemary, and onion and garlic powder. Mix half of the sun-dried tomatoes with the yogurt, eggs and sun-dried tomato paste or purée in another bowl or jug. Pour the wet ingredients into the dry ingredients and stir with a large spoon until just combined.

- Divide the mixture between the holes in the tin, then top with the remaining sun-dried tomatoes and grated cheese. Bake in the preheated oven for 18–20 minutes, or until a skewer inserted into one of the muffins comes out clean. Cool for a few minutes on a wire rack, then serve.

---

1 **Toasted Tomato and Rosemary Muffins** Split 4 English muffins in half and lay, cut side up, on a baking sheet. Spread each half with 2 tablespoons sun-dried tomato paste and sprinkle with 1 teaspoon dried rosemary and 3 tablespoons grated Parmesan or Cheddar. Cook under a preheated grill for 3–4 minutes. Meanwhile, slice 3 tomatoes and 125 g (4 oz) mozzarella cheese, arrange on 4 plates and drizzle with a little groundnut oil. Place the muffins on the plates and serve drizzled with balsamic vinegar, if desired.

2 **Tomato, Rosemary and Garlic Pizza Bread** Place 50 g (2 oz) sun-dried tomatoes, chopped, and 2 tablespoons sun-dried tomato paste in a mini-chopper or the small bowl of a food processor with 1 large crushed garlic clove and 100 g (3½ oz) slightly softened butter. Blend until smooth, then stir in 1 teaspoon dried rosemary and 2 tablespoons grated Parmesan-style cheese. Spread the paste over 2 ready-made pizza bases, approximately 25 cm (10 inches) in diameter, and place on 1 or 2 baking sheets. Cook in a preheated oven, 180°C (350°F), Gas Mark 4, for 10–12 minutes until melted and lightly golden. Serve in wedges as a starter or snack.

Chorizo and Red Pepper Tortilla

Serves 4

2 tablespoons olive oil

250 g (8 oz) cooking chorizo, diced

1 large red onion, halved and sliced

2 garlic cloves, chopped

1 teaspoon hot smoked paprika

½ teaspoon dried thyme

1 teaspoon dried oregano

375 g (12 oz) roasted red peppers
from a jar, drained and rinsed,
cut into strips

6 eggs, lightly beaten

2 tablespoons chopped flat leaf
parsley

125 g (4 oz) Cheddar cheese,
grated

freshly ground black pepper

- Heat the oil in a large nonstick frying pan and add the chorizo and onion. Cook gently for 2–3 minutes, then stir in the garlic. Cook for 4–5 minutes, until softened. Stir in the spices and dried herbs, and cook for a further 2 minutes, then add the peppers.

- Beat the eggs with the parsley and season with black pepper. Pour the egg mixture into the pan and cook gently for 3–4 minutes, stirring occasionally to prevent the base from burning, until the egg is almost set.

- Sprinkle with the grated Cheddar, then slide under a hot grill, keeping the handle away from the heat. Grill for 2–3 minutes, until golden and set. Slice into wedges and serve immediately.

---

10 Chorizo and Red Pepper Bagels

Split 4 bagels and toast until lightly golden. Place, cut side up, on a baking sheet and top with 75 g (3 oz) thinly sliced chorizo, 200 g (7 oz) roasted red peppers from a jar, drained and sliced, 125 g (4 oz) grated Cheddar cheese and 1 teaspoon dried oregano. Cook under a preheated grill for 4–5 minutes, until bubbling. Meanwhile, heat 1 tablespoon of olive oil in a frying pan until very hot, and break 4 small eggs into the pan. Fry for 2–3 minutes, until the white is set but the yolk is still runny. Arrange the bagels on 4 plates and top each with a fried egg and a sprinkle of black pepper.

30 Baked Eggs with Chorizo and Red Peppers

Heat 2 tablespoons olive oil in a large, ovenproof frying pan and add 250 g (8 oz) cooking chorizo, diced, and 1 large red onion, halved and thinly sliced. Cook gently for 2–3 minutes, then stir in 2 garlic cloves, chopped. Cook for 4–5 minutes, until softened. Stir in 1 teaspoon each of hot smoked paprika and dried oregano, ½ teaspoon dried thyme, 375 g (12 oz) roasted red peppers (from a jar), drained and rinsed, and 4 large ripe tomatoes, diced. Cook gently for 7–8 minutes, until the tomatoes have softened.

Divide the tomato mixture between 4 individual ovenproof dishes, then crack an egg into the centre of each one. Season with black pepper and cook in a preheated oven, 200°C (400°F), Gas Mark 6, for 8–10 minutes or until the egg white is set but the yolk is still slightly runny. Serve with crusty bread.

Tandoori Chicken Wings with Raita

Serves 4

2 tablespoons tandoori paste
1 teaspoon cumin seeds
75 ml (3 fl oz) natural yogurt
2 teaspoons lemon juice
8–12 chicken wings, about 750 g
   (1½ lb) total weight

For the raita

150 g (5 oz) cucumber
200 ml (7 fl oz) natural yogurt
2 teaspoons lemon juice
½ teaspoon ground cumin
salt and pepper

To serve

½ iceberg lettuce, shredded
4–8 poppadoms (optional)

- Preheat the oven to 220°C (425°F), Gas Mark 7, and line a baking sheet with foil. Mix the tandoori paste, cumin seeds, yogurt and lemon juice in a large, shallow dish. Make 2–3 shallow cuts in each chicken wing and place in the dish. Use your fingers to coat the chicken wings thoroughly with the tandoori yogurt.

- Arrange the wings in a single layer on the prepared baking sheet and cook in the preheated oven for 20–25 minutes, until slightly charred and the juices run clear when the thickest part of the chicken is pierced with a fork.

- In the meantime, make the raita. Halve the piece of cucumber lengthways and use a spoon to remove the seeds. Coarsely grate the flesh and place in the middle of a clean tea towel, then bring up the edges and twist the cucumber in the tea towel over a sink to squeeze out the excess moisture. Place the cucumber in a bowl, add the yogurt, lemon juice and ground cumin, then season to taste and chill until the chicken is cooked.

- Serve the cooked chicken wings with the shredded lettuce, cool raita and crisp poppadoms, if using.

Tandoori Chicken Pittas

Mix 1 tablespoon tandoori paste in a bowl with 150 ml (¼ pint) natural yogurt, 1 tablespoon chopped mint, ½ teaspoon ground cumin, 2 teaspoons lemon juice and plenty of salt and pepper. Fold in 300 g (10 oz) diced, cooked chicken and stir thoroughly to coat, then spoon into 4 large, warmed wholemeal pitta breads. Add some shredded lettuce and serve immediately.

Grilled Tandoori Chicken with Raita

Place 4 chicken breasts, about 625 g (1¼ lb) total weight, one at a time between 2 large pieces of clingfilm and beat with a rolling pin to flatten slightly. Mix 2 tablespoons tandoori paste with 4 tablespoons natural yogurt, and rub all over the chicken breasts. Set aside to marinate for 8–10 minutes. Meanwhile, prepare the raita following the main recipe. Place the chicken breasts on a foil-lined grill rack and cook under a preheated grill for 7–8 minutes, turning once, until cooked through. Remove from the grill, slice thickly and serve with ½ iceberg lettuce, shredded, the raita and 4–8 crisp poppadoms, if desired.

Creamy Baked Eggs with Blue Cheese

Serves 4

butter, for greasing and spreading
75 g (3 oz) blue cheese, such as
   Stilton, Roquefort or Gorgonzola
150 ml (¼ pint) double cream
2 tablespoons chopped chives
½ teaspoon cracked black pepper
4 large eggs
4 slices of granary bread

· Preheat the oven to 200°C (400°F), Gas Mark 6, and butter 4 ramekins. In a small bowl, mash the blue cheese into the cream using the back of a fork. Stir in the chives and black pepper, and divide between the ramekins.

· Crack an egg into each ramekin and place them in a roasting tin. Pour hot water into the tin so that it comes about halfway up the sides of the ramekins. Cook in the preheated oven for 7–8 minutes, or until the egg white is set but the yolk is still runny.

· Meanwhile, toast the bread until golden and butter lightly. Cut into strips for dipping. Remove the baked eggs from the oven and serve immediately with the toast.

Creamy Scrambled Eggs with Blue Cheese Beat 8 eggs in a bowl with 75 ml (3 fl oz) full-fat milk and plenty of black pepper. Melt 1 tablespoon butter in a large nonstick saucepan until frothy, then pour in the eggs. Once the eggs begin to set, use a heat-resistant rubber spatula to fold gently over a very low heat for 5–6 minutes, until the eggs are creamy and lightly set. Remove from the heat and crumble over 75 g (3 oz) blue cheese and 2 tablespoons chopped chives. Serve the eggs spooned over 4 slices of hot, buttered toast.

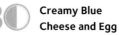

Creamy Blue Cheese and Egg Pie Grease a shallow pie dish, approximately 23 cm (9 inches) across and 2.5 cm (1 inch) deep, and line with a sheet of ready-rolled shortcrust pastry. Squeeze the excess moisture from 300 g (10 oz) defrosted leaf spinach and place in a bowl with 100 ml (3½ fl oz) double cream, 2 tablespoons chives, 4 large eggs and plenty of black pepper. Stir to just combine, then pour the mixture into the pastry shell. Cover with a second sheet of pastry and squeeze together the edges to seal, trimming off any excess pastry.

Brush with beaten egg and cut 2 little slits in the centre of the pie. Cook in a preheated oven, 200°C (400°F), Gas Mark 6, for about 22 minutes, until the pastry is crisp and golden.

 # Lemon and Spinach Soup with White Rice

Serves 4

2 tablespoons olive or
  vegetable oil

1 large onion, finely chopped

2 garlic cloves, finely chopped

175 g (6 oz) long-grain
  white rice, rinsed

1.2 litres (2 pints) clear
  chicken stock

4 tablespoons lemon juice

3 large eggs, beaten

200 g (7 oz) spinach leaves,
  rinsed and chopped

salt and pepper

To serve

2 tablespoons chopped parsley

2 tablespoons grated Parmesan-
  style cheese

- Heat the oil in a large saucepan or casserole, and cook the onion and garlic gently for 7–8 minutes, until softened. Stir in the rice and cook for 1 minute, then pour in the chicken stock. Simmer gently for 12–15 minutes, until the rice is just tender. Remove from the heat.

- In a small bowl, whisk the lemon juice with the beaten eggs and a pinch of salt. Continue whisking while you add a ladleful of hot stock in a slow, steady stream, then whisk the egg mixture into the saucepan of soup. Return the pan to a very low heat, and continue stirring for 2–3 minutes, until the soup has thickened slightly, taking care not to allow it to boil.

- Stir in the chopped spinach and season to taste, then ladle the soup into 4 bowls. Serve scattered with chopped parsley and grated cheese.

1 Quick Lemon and Spinach Soup

Heat 1 litre (1¾ pints) chicken stock to boiling point in a large saucepan. Add 500 g (1 lb) cooked rice, stir until heated through, then remove from the heat. In a small bowl, whisk 4 tablespoons lemon juice with 3 large eggs and a pinch of salt. Continue whisking while you add a ladleful of hot stock in a slow, steady stream, then whisk the egg mixture into the saucepan of soup to thicken. Stir in 200 g (7 oz) spinach leaves, rinsed and chopped, and serve.

2 Creamy Lemon and Chicken Rice

Heat 2 tablespoons olive or vegetable oil in a large, deep-sided frying pan and cook 375 g (12 oz) diced chicken breast or thigh over a medium-high heat for 6–7 minutes, until golden. Reduce the heat, add 1 large onion, finely chopped, and 2 garlic cloves, finely chopped, and cook for 4–5 minutes, until softened and lightly golden. Stir in 4 tablespoons lemon juice and 100 ml (3½ fl oz) hot chicken stock, and simmer gently for 2–3 minutes, until the chicken is just cooked through. Pour 275 ml (9 fl oz) double cream into the pan, then season to taste. Stir in 200 g (7 oz) spinach leaves, rinsed and chopped, and heat until just wilted. Serve immediately with 500 g (1 lb) cooked rice.

Cauliflower Coleslaw Pockets

Serves 4

½ small cauliflower, cut into
  small florets
1 carrot, peeled and grated
1 celery stick, thinly sliced
2 spring onions, thinly sliced
4 tablespoons mayonnaise
1 teaspoon chipotle paste or
  sun-dried tomato paste
1 tablespoon red wine vinegar
½ teaspoon caster sugar
salt and pepper
4 large, warmed, wholemeal pitta
  breads, to serve

- Combine the cauliflower, carrot, celery and spring onion in a large bowl. In a separate bowl, mix together the mayonnaise, chipotle paste, vinegar and sugar, and season to taste with salt and pepper.

- Add the dressing to the vegetables and mix until really well coated. Spoon the mixture into the pitta breads and serve immediately.

---

20 Pan-Roasted Cauliflower and Chickpea Salad

Heat 2 tablespoons oil in a frying pan. Add 2 spring onions, thinly sliced, and cook for 1 minute, until just softened. Add ¼ small cauliflower, cut into small florets, then chop 1 celery stick and 1 peeled carrot, and add to the pan with 1 teaspoon chipotle paste or 2 tablespoons sun-dried tomato paste. Fry for 1–2 minutes before adding 1 tablespoon red vinegar and 175 ml (6 fl oz) vegetable stock. Cover and simmer gently for 5–6 minutes, until just tender but still with some 'bite'. Add a 400 g (13 oz) can chickpeas, drained, and cook for 1–2 minutes, stirring occasionally. Spoon into bowls and serve with warmed pittas.

30 Spicy Roast Cauliflower

Place ½ small cauliflower, cut into small florets, in a large bowl, then cut 1 peeled carrot, 1 celery stick and 2 spring onions into bite-sized pieces. Toss with 2 tablespoons olive or vegetable oil, 1 teaspoon chipotle or sun-dried tomato paste, 1 tablespoon red wine vinegar and 1 teaspoon honey. Season and tip into a large roasting tin. Cook in a preheated oven, 200°C (400°F), Gas Mark 6, for 20–25 minutes, until just tender and golden, but still with some bite. For a more substantial meal, toss with 250 g (8 oz) cooked couscous and serve with warmed pitta breads and 4 tablespoons natural yogurt.

 # Tofu Ramen Noodle Soup

Serves 4

25 g (1 oz) dried whole shiitake
  mushrooms
1.2 litres (2 pints) vegetable stock
1–2 tablespoons light soy sauce,
  plus extra to serve
200 g (7 oz) dried ramen or
  egg noodles
375 g (12 oz) firm tofu, sliced
200 g (7 oz) bean sprouts
2 spring onions, finely sliced

- Place the mushrooms in a pan with the vegetable stock, cover, bring to the boil, then simmer gently for about 15 minutes, until softened. Remove with a slotted spoon, cool slightly, then slice the fleshy parts thickly and return to the pan, discarding the tough stalks. Season the soup to taste with soy sauce.

- Meanwhile, bring a large saucepan of water to the boil, add the noodles and immediately remove from the heat. Cover and set aside for 4–5 minutes, until tender. Alternatively, cook according to packet instructions, then heap into 4 warmed bowls.

- Top the noodles with the slices of tofu and bean sprouts, then ladle over the hot mushrooms and broth. Scatter over the spring onions and serve immediately, with extra soy sauce, if desired.

Mushroom Noodle Stir-Fry

Heat 2 tablespoons vegetable oil in a large frying pan or wok, add 1 tablespoon chopped fresh root ginger and 2 chopped garlic cloves, and cook for 1–2 minutes, until softened. Add 350 g (11½ oz) sliced button mushrooms and stir-fry for 3–4 minutes, until almost tender. Stir in 325 g (11 oz) ready-made stir-fry sauce and heat until just simmering. Spoon the mushroom mixture over 400 g (13 oz) hot, cooked egg noodles, and serve immediately.

Vegetable Noodle Soup

Simmer 25 g (1 oz) dried whole shiitake mushrooms in 750 ml (1¼ pints) hot vegetable stock in a saucepan, following the main recipe, then slice as above and set aside. Heat 2 tablespoons vegetable oil in a frying pan or wok, and stir-fry 2 spring onions, finely sliced, with 1 tablespoon chopped fresh root ginger and 2 chopped garlic cloves for 1–2 minutes, until softened. Add the sliced shiitake mushrooms to the pan and stir-fry for 2–3 minutes, before adding 200 g (7 oz) bean sprouts and 100 g (3½ oz) thinly sliced mangetout, and cooking for a further 1–2 minutes. Add 350 ml (12 fl oz) of the hot mushroom stock to the pan and season to taste with 1–2 tablespoons light soy sauce. Add 300 g (10 oz) straight-to-wok udon or egg noodles, cook until hot, then heap into bowls and spoon over the soupy broth. Serve topped with 375 g (12 oz) firm tofu, sliced, if desired.

Courgette and Bacon Carbonara Frittata

Serves 4

250 g (8 oz) spaghetti
25 g (1 oz) butter
1 tablespoon olive or vegetable oil
150 g (5 oz) smoked bacon, chopped
375 g (12 oz) courgettes, coarsely grated
2 garlic cloves, chopped
4 large eggs, lightly beaten
100 ml (3½ fl oz) single cream
50 g (2 oz) Parmesan-style cheese, grated
salt and pepper

- Cook the spaghetti according to packet instructions. Meanwhile, melt the butter with the oil in a large, nonstick frying pan and add the bacon. Cook for 4–5 minutes, until golden.

- Place the courgettes in the middle of a clean tea towel, bring up the edges and twist the tea towel over a sink to squeeze out the excess moisture. Add to the bacon with the garlic, and cook for a further 4–5 minutes, until soft and golden. Meanwhile, mix the beaten eggs in a jug with the cream, half the cheese and plenty of seasoning.

- Transfer the courgette and bacon to a large mixing bowl, then toss with the drained pasta and egg mixture. Return to the frying pan and cook over a medium-low heat for 5–6 minutes. Sprinkle with the remaining cheese, then slide under a hot grill, keeping the handle away from the heat. Grill for 4–5 minutes, until golden and set. Slice into wedges and serve immediately.

Courgette and Bacon Carbonara

Heat 25 g (1 oz) butter and 1 tablespoon oil in a frying pan and cook 150 g (5 oz) chopped smoked bacon for 3–4 minutes. Meanwhile, cook 400 g (13 oz) quick-cook spaghetti according to packet instructions. Prepare 200 g (7 oz) grated courgettes as above, add to the bacon with 2 chopped garlic cloves, and cook for 3–4 minutes. Meanwhile, beat 2 egg yolks and 2 eggs in a bowl with 275 ml (9 fl oz) single cream, 50 g (2 oz) grated Parmesan and black pepper. Return the drained pasta to the pan, toss with the courgette, bacon and egg mixture.

Courgette and Bacon Carbonara

Bake Cook 300 g (10 oz) pasta shapes in a large saucepan of lightly salted boiling water for 11 minutes, or according to packet instructions, until al dente. Meanwhile, cook 150 g (5 oz) smoked bacon, chopped, 375 g (12 oz) courgettes, coarsely grated, and 2 garlic cloves, chopped, following the main recipe. Beat 2 egg yolks and 2 eggs in a bowl with 275 ml (9 fl oz) single cream, 50 g (2 oz) grated Parmesan-style cheese and plenty of black pepper. Drain the pasta, return to the pan and toss with the courgette, bacon and egg mixture, until well coated. Transfer to a large, shallow ovenproof dish and sprinkle with a further 50 g (2 oz) grated cheese. Cook under a preheated grill for 7–8 minutes, until the cheesy topping is golden. Serve with green salad.

 # Roasted Chickpeas with Spinach

Serves 4

400 g (13 oz) can chickpeas, drained and rinsed

3 tablespoons olive or vegetable oil

1 teaspoon cumin seeds

1 teaspoon paprika

½ red onion, thinly sliced

3 ripe tomatoes, roughly chopped

100 g (3½ oz) young spinach leaves

2 tablespoons lemon juice

100 g (3½ oz) feta cheese (optional)

lemon wedges, to garnish

salt and pepper

- Preheat the oven to 220°C (425°F), Gas Mark 7. Mix the chickpeas in a bowl with 1 tablespoon oil, the cumin seeds and the paprika, and season with salt and pepper. Tip into a large nonstick roasting tin and roast in the preheated oven for 12–15 minutes, until nutty and golden.

- Meanwhile, place the onion and tomatoes in a large bowl with the spinach leaves and toss gently to combine. Heap on to 4 serving plates.

- Remove the chickpeas from the oven and scatter over the spinach salad. Crumble the feta over the top, if using, and drizzle each plate with the lemon juice and remaining olive oil. Garnish with lemon wedges and serve immediately.

 ### Chickpea and Spinach Salad

Toss 400 g (13 oz) can chickpeas, drained and rinsed, with 3 tablespoons olive or vegetable oil and 1 teaspoon each of cumin seeds and paprika. Season with salt and pepper. Tip into a large frying pan and heat for 2–3 minutes, stirring occasionally, until hot and fragrant. Remove from the heat, toss with ½ red onion, thinly sliced, and 3 ripe tomatoes, roughly chopped, and fold into 100 g (3½ oz) young spinach leaves, torn. Heap on to serving plates and serve with 100 g (3½ oz) feta cheese, crumbled, if desired.

Aromatic Chickpea and Spinach Stew

Heat 2 tablespoons olive or vegetable oil in a large, deep-sided frying pan or casserole. Chop 1 red onion, 2 large garlic cloves and a 1.5-cm (¾-inch) piece of fresh root ginger. Add to the pan and cook gently for about 10 minutes, until softened and lightly golden. Add 1 teaspoon each of cumin seeds and paprika, and cook for a further minute, then add 4 large, ripe, diced tomatoes, 400 g (13 oz) can chickpeas, drained and rinsed, 2 tablespoons lemon juice and 125 ml (4 fl oz) hot water or vegetable stock. Bring to the boil, reduce the heat and simmer gently, covered, for 12–15 minutes, until softened and thickened. Season to taste, then stir in 100 g (3½ oz) young spinach leaves, torn, and cook gently until wilted. Spoon into 4 shallow bowls and serve scattered with 2 tablespoons chopped parsley and 100 g (3½ oz) feta cheese, crumbled, if desired.

Storecupboard Spicy Bean Soup

Serves 4

2 tablespoons vegetable oil

1 large onion, chopped

1 red pepper, cored, deseeded and chopped

2 garlic cloves, chopped

30 g (1¼ oz) sachet Mexican fajita, taco, or chilli con carne spice mix

400 g (13 oz) can kidney beans, drained and rinsed

400 g (13 oz) can black beans, drained and rinsed

400 g (13 oz) can tomatoes

750 ml (1¼ pints) boiling water

1 beef or vegetable stock cube

To serve

4 tablespoons soured cream

25 g (1 oz) tortilla chips (optional)

- Heat the vegetable oil in a large, heavy-based saucepan or casserole, and cook the onion and pepper over a medium-high heat for 4 minutes. Add the garlic and fry for a further 2 minutes, until lightly coloured.

- Stir in the spice mix, then add half of the beans, the chopped tomatoes, measured water and stock cube. Stir well, bring to the boil and simmer for 10–12 minutes, until slightly thickened.

- Use a hand-held blender to blend the soup until almost smooth, then stir in the remaining beans and heat through. Ladle into 4 deep bowls and serve immediately with a drizzle of soured cream and a scattering of tortilla chips, if desired.

Spicy Bean Tacos Heat 2 tablespoons oil in a large saucepan and cook 1 large onion, chopped, and 1 red pepper, cored, deseeded and chopped, for 4 minutes. Add 2 garlic cloves, chopped, and fry for a further 2 minutes. Add 30 g (1¼ oz) sachet Mexican fajita, taco, or chilli con carne spice mix, 400 g (13 oz) can each of kidney beans and black beans, 2 diced tomatoes and 75 ml (3 fl oz) water. Simmer for 2–3 minutes, then spoon into 8 warmed taco shells and serve immediately with 4 tablespoons soured cream.

Spicy Bean Enchiladas Follow the 10-minute recipe to make the spicy bean mixture, then divide it between 8 small, soft flour tortillas and scatter over 75 g (3 oz) grated Cheddar or mozzarella cheese. Tuck in the ends and roll each tortilla tightly, then place in a snug-fitting ovenproof dish. Pour a 300 g (10 oz) jar of hot Mexican salsa over the tortillas and scatter over a further 75 g (3 oz) grated cheese. Cook in a preheated oven, 200°C (400°F), Gas Mark 6, for about 15 minutes until hot and bubbling. Serve with 4 tablespoons soured cream.

QuickCook

Veggie Delights

Recipes listed by cooking time

30

20

10

Creamy Mushroom and Tarragon Rigatoni

Serves 4

50 g (2 oz) butter
1 tablespoon olive or vegetable oil
1 large leek, thinly sliced
1 garlic clove, chopped
150 g (5 oz) mushrooms, sliced
1 teaspoon dried tarragon
400 g (13 oz) rigatoni or
   tortiglioni pasta
100 ml (3½ fl oz) dry white wine
   or vegetable stock
250 ml (8 fl oz) single cream
salt and pepper
4 teaspoons grated Parmesan-
   style cheese, to serve

- Heat the butter and oil in a large nonstick frying pan until the butter is frothing. Add the leek and garlic, and cook for 2–3 minutes, until beginning to soften. Add the mushrooms and tarragon, and cook for a further 4–5 minutes, until soft and golden.

- Meanwhile, cook the pasta in a large saucepan of lightly salted boiling water for 11 minutes, or according to packet instructions, until al dente.

- Pour the white wine and cream into the mushrooms, and season generously with salt and pepper. Simmer gently for 6–7 minutes.

- Drain the pasta and stir into the sauce. Spoon into 4 shallow bowls and serve immediately, sprinkled with grated Parmesan.

Quick Creamy Mushroom Penne

Heat 50 g (2 oz) butter and 1 tablespoon oil in a large frying pan. Add 1 thinly sliced large leek and 1 chopped garlic clove, and cook for 2–3 minutes. Add 150 g (5 oz) sliced mushrooms and 1 tablespoon chopped fresh tarragon, and cook for a further 4–5 minutes. Cook 400 g (13 oz) quick-cook penne pasta according to packet instructions. Stir 150 g (5 oz) cream cheese and 8 sliced sun-dried tomatoes into the mushrooms with 250 ml (8 fl oz) single cream, then bring to the boil and season. Pour over the drained pasta and serve with 4 teaspoons grated Parmesan-style cheese.

Creamy-Topped Mushroom Bake

Make the sauce following the 10-minute recipe, but use 1 teaspoon dried tarragon instead of the fresh tarragon. Cook 350 g (11½ oz) quick-cook penne pasta in a large saucepan of lightly salted boiling water, and drain after 3 minutes. Meanwhile, beat 1 egg and 1 egg yolk with 4 teaspoons grated Parmesan-style cheese and 300 ml (½ pint) Greek yogurt, then season lightly and set aside. Stir the pasta into the mushroom sauce and then transfer to a large ovenproof dish. Top with the egg and yogurt mixture, then cook in a preheated oven, 200°C (400°F), Gas Mark 6, for about 20 minutes until bubbling and golden. Serve with crusty bread.

Courgette and Garlic Chilli Fusilli

Serves 4

400 g (13 oz) quick-cook fusilli pasta

300 g (10 oz) courgettes, coarsely grated

4 tablespoons olive or vegetable oil

1 red chilli, finely chopped

2 garlic cloves, finely chopped

2 tablespoons lemon juice

3 tablespoons chopped flat leaf parsley (optional)

salt and pepper

50 g (2 oz) Parmesan-style cheese, grated, to serve (optional)

- Cook the pasta in a large saucepan of lightly salted boiling water for 4–5 minutes, or according to packet instructions, until al dente.

- Meanwhile, place the courgettes in the middle of a clean tea towel, bring up the edges and twist the courgettes in the tea towel over a sink to squeeze out the excess moisture.

- Heat the oil in a nonstick frying pan with the chilli and garlic, and cook gently for 1 minute, until the oil is fragrant. Increase the heat slightly and add the courgettes. Cook gently for 5–6 minutes, until soft and golden.

- Drain the pasta and stir in the courgette mixture, lemon juice and parsley, if using. Season to taste with salt and pepper, and serve immediately with the cheese, if using.

2 **Courgette and Garlic Cheat's Risotto** Heat 4 tablespoons olive or vegetable oil in a nonstick frying pan with 1 finely chopped red chilli and 2 finely chopped garlic cloves, and cook gently for 1 minute, until the oil is fragrant. Increase the heat, add 300 g (10 oz) coarsely grated courgettes and fry for 3–4 minutes, until just golden, then stir in 250 g (8 oz) orzo (rice-shaped pasta). Alternatively, use giant couscous or small pasta shapes. Add 500 ml (17 fl oz) hot vegetable stock and plenty of seasoning, and bring to the boil. Reduce the heat, cover with a lid and cook for about 10 minutes, until the liquid has been absorbed and the pasta is tender. Use a fork to stir through 3 tablespoons chopped flat leaf parsley and 2 tablespoons lemon juice, then check the seasoning and serve with grated cheese, if desired.

3 **Crispy-Topped Courgette and Garlic Bake** Follow the main recipe, using only 2 tablespoons parsley. Stir 250 g (8 oz) mascarpone into the pasta, season to taste and transfer to a large, ovenproof dish. Mix 75 g (3 oz) fresh breadcrumbs with 50 g (2 oz) grated Parmesan-style cheese and the remaining tablespoon of parsley, and sprinkle over the pasta. Cook in a preheated oven, 190°C (375°F), Gas Mark 5, for 15–20 minutes until bubbling and golden. Serve with green salad.

Gardener's Pie

Serves 4

750 g (1½ lb) small new potatoes
3 tablespoons olive or
   vegetable oil
1 onion, chopped
1 celery stick, chopped
2 garlic cloves, chopped
3 tablespoons ready-made pesto
500 g (1 lb) ripe tomatoes, diced
150 ml (¼ pint) hot vegetable
   stock or water
400 g (13 oz) can borlotti
   or haricot beans, drained
   and rinsed
125 g (4 oz) fresh or defrosted
   green beans, cut into 2.5-cm
   (1-inch) lengths
50 g (2 oz) Parmesan-style
   cheese, grated
salt and pepper

- Cook the new potatoes in a saucepan of lightly salted boiling water for about 10 minutes, until just tender. Drain and cool slightly, then cut into 5-mm (¼-inch) slices.

- Meanwhile, heat 2 tablespoons of oil in a large, deep-sided frying pan and cook the onion for 2 minutes. Add the celery and cook for a further 2 minutes, then add the garlic and cook for a final 2–3 minutes, stirring frequently, until lightly golden.

- Stir the pesto into the onions, then add the diced tomatoes, stock, borlotti beans and green beans. Season generously with salt and pepper and bring to the boil, reduce the heat and simmer for 5 minutes, until the tomatoes soften and the beans are tender.

- Tip the vegetable mixture into a large ovenproof dish, and arrange the sliced potatoes over the top. Sprinkle with the grated cheese, drizzle with the remaining oil and cook under a preheated grill for 7–8 minutes, until golden.

1 **Quick Gardener's Salad** Coarsely grate 2 carrots, and thinly slice 2 celery sticks. Toss with 400 g (13 oz) can borlotti or haricot beans, drained and rinsed, and 500 g (1 lb) diced ripe tomatoes, and divide between 4 serving bowls. Mix 2 tablespoons ready-made pesto with 2 tablespoons oil and 1 tablespoon balsamic vinegar. Season to taste, and drizzle over the salad to serve.

2 **Gardener's Curry** Heat 2 tablespoons vegetable oil in a heavy-based casserole over a medium-high heat, and fry 1 chopped onion, 1 chopped celery stick and 2 chopped garlic cloves for 5–6 minutes, until lightly coloured. Stir in 4 tablespoons medium jalfrezi curry paste, and cook gently for 2 minutes. Add 500 g (1 lb) diced ripe tomatoes, a 400 g (13 oz) can lentils in water, drained, and 200 ml (7 fl oz) hot water or vegetable stock, and simmer gently, uncovered, for about 10 minutes, until thickened and fragrant. Serve hot in shallow bowls with warmed naan bread.

 Sweet Potato and Coconut Rice

Serves 4

3 tablespoons vegetable oil

625 g (1¼ lb) sweet potato, cut
into 1.5-cm (¾-inch) cubes

2.5-cm (1-inch) piece of fresh
root ginger, peeled and
finely chopped

2 garlic cloves, thinly sliced

1 teaspoon cumin seeds

1 red chilli, deseeded and chopped
(optional)

250 g (8 oz) long-grain rice

350 ml (12 fl oz) hot vegetable
stock

200 ml (7 fl oz) coconut milk

2 tablespoons coconut shavings
or desiccated coconut

salt and pepper

- Heat the oil in a large nonstick saucepan or casserole with a tight-fitting lid. Add the sweet potato, ginger, garlic, cumin seeds and chilli, if using, and fry gently for 5–6 minutes, until lightly golden.

- Add the rice and stir for a minute until well coated. Pour in the hot stock and coconut milk, and bring to the boil. Reduce the heat, season generously with salt and pepper and cover with the lid. Simmer gently for 15–17 minutes, until the liquid has been absorbed and the rice and potatoes are tender.

- Meanwhile, toast the coconut in a dry frying pan for 3–4 minutes, until golden. Tip on to a plate to cool.

- Fluff up the rice with a fork and spoon into shallow bowls. Scatter with the toasted coconut, and serve immediately.

1 **Aromatic Coconut Rice**
Heat 3 tablespoons vegetable oil in a large, nonstick frying pan, and fry 2.5-cm (1-inch) piece of fresh root ginger, peeled and finely chopped, 2 sliced garlic cloves, 1 teaspoon cumin seeds and 1 deseeded and chopped red chilli, if using, for 2–3 minutes. Stir in 500 g (1 lb) cooked rice and 200 ml (7 fl oz) coconut milk. Stir over a medium heat for 2–3 minutes, until the rice is hot and sticky. Serve with 2 tablespoons toasted coconut shavings and steamed broccoli.

2 **Curried Sweet Potato and Coconut Soup** Heat 3 tablespoons vegetable oil in a large nonstick saucepan or casserole. Add 625 g (1¼ lb) cubed sweet potato, 2.5-cm (1-inch) piece of fresh root ginger, peeled and finely chopped, 2 thinly sliced garlic cloves, 1 teaspoon cumin seeds and 1 deseeded and chopped red chilli, if using, and fry gently for 5–6 minutes, until lightly golden. Add 2 tablespoons Thai red curry paste and 400 ml (14 fl oz) coconut milk and cook for 2 minutes. Add 1 litre (1¾ pints) hot vegetable stock, then bring to the boil and simmer gently for about 12 minutes, until the potato is tender. Use a hand-held blender to blend the soup until smooth, and ladle into deep bowls. Serve scattered with 2 tablespoons toasted coconut shavings.

Bulgar Wheat with Goats' Cheese and Red Onion

Serves 4

750 ml (1¼ pints) hot vegetable stock
275 g (9 oz) bulgar wheat
4 tablespoons olive or vegetable oil
1 large red onion, halved and thinly sliced
100 ml (3½ fl oz) tomato juice
2 tablespoons lime juice
175 g (6 oz) firm goats' cheese, crumbled
3 tablespoons roughly chopped flat leaf parsley
salt and pepper

- Bring the vegetable stock to the boil in a large saucepan, add the bulgar wheat and cook for 7 minutes. Remove from the heat, cover with a tight-fitting lid and set aside for 5–8 minutes, until the liquid has been absorbed and the grains are tender.

- Meanwhile, heat 2 tablespoons of oil in a frying pan and cook the onion gently for 7–8 minutes, until soft and golden.

- Combine the remaining oil with the tomato juice and lime juice, and season with salt and pepper. Fold the dressing, onion, goats' cheese and parsley into the bulgar wheat with a fork, and spoon into 4 shallow bowls to serve.

Goats' Cheese Couscous Place 250 g (8 oz) couscous in a bowl with 1 tablespoon of olive or vegetable oil and a generous pinch of salt. Pour over 300 ml (½ pint) boiling vegetable stock and set aside for 5–8 minutes, until the grains are tender and the liquid has been absorbed. Meanwhile, combine 3 tablespoons oil with 100 ml (3½ fl oz) tomato juice and 2 tablespoons lime juice, and season with salt and pepper. Fold the goats' cheese and parsley into the couscous and spoon into serving bowls. Drizzle with the dressing and scatter with 3 sliced spring onions to serve.

Goats' Cheese Parcels with Bulgar Salad Roll 500 g (1 lb) ready-made puff pastry out into a 30-cm (12-inch) square, then cut into quarters. Crumble 175 g (6 oz) firm goats' cheese and place some cheese in the centre of each square, then divide 8 halved cherry tomatoes and 2 thinly sliced spring onions between them. Fold the sides of the pastry squares in towards the centre, so that the filling is not quite covered, and pinch together the sides to seal. Cook in a preheated oven, 180°C (350°F), Gas Mark 4, for 18–20 minutes, until crisp and golden. Meanwhile, prepare the bulgar wheat following the main recipe but omitting the goats' cheese. Spoon the bulgar on to 4 serving plates and serve with the goats' cheese parcels.

Chickpea and Spinach Omelette

Serves 4

2 tablespoons olive oil

1 large onion, sliced

1 red pepper, sliced

½ teaspoon hot smoked or sweet paprika

400 g (13 oz) can chickpeas, drained and rinsed

100 g (3½ oz) spinach leaves, rinsed and roughly sliced

5 eggs, lightly beaten

75 g (3 oz) pitted green olives, roughly chopped

150 g (5 oz) Cheddar cheese, grated

salt and pepper

- Heat the olive oil in a large nonstick frying pan. Add the onion and pepper and cook gently for 7–8 minutes, until soft and golden. Stir in the paprika and chickpeas, and cook for 1 minute, stirring frequently. Add the spinach leaves and cook until just wilted.

- Pour the beaten eggs into the pan and stir to combine. Cook gently, without stirring, for 4–5 minutes, until almost set.

- Sprinkle with the olives and grated Cheddar, then slide under a hot grill, keeping the handle away from the heat. Grill for 4–5 minutes, until golden and set. Slice into wedges and serve immediately.

10 Chickpea and Spinach Salad with Poached Eggs

Heat 2 tablespoons olive oil in a large frying pan. Add 1 sliced onion and 1 sliced red pepper, and cook gently for 7–8 minutes. Stir in ½ teaspoon hot smoked or sweet paprika and 400 g (13 oz) can chickpeas, drained and rinsed, and cook for 1 minute, stirring frequently. Meanwhile, poach 4 eggs in a large pan of gently simmering water. Toss the chickpea mixture briefly with 200 g (7 oz) baby spinach leaves and heap on to 4 serving plates. Top each salad with a poached egg and serve immediately.

30 Chickpea Casserole with Garlic Bread

Heat 2 tablespoons olive oil in a large nonstick frying pan. Cook 1 large sliced onion and 1 sliced red pepper gently for 4–5 minutes, then add 2 chopped garlic cloves and cook for a further 3 minutes, until soft and golden. Stir in a 400 g (13 oz) can chopped tomatoes, 150 ml (¼ pint) hot water or vegetable stock, 400 g (13 oz) can chickpeas, drained and rinsed, and 75 g (3 oz) roughly chopped pitted green olives, and simmer gently for 12–15 minutes, until thick and rich. Meanwhile, wash, trim and roughly slice 250 g (8 oz) spinach leaves and cook 8 garlic bread slices according to packet instructions. Stir the spinach into the chickpeas and cook for 1–2 minutes, until just wilted, then season to taste with salt and pepper. Spoon into 4 bowls and serve with the hot, crusty garlic bread.

 # Chilli con Verduda

Serves 4

2 tablespoons vegetable oil
1 carrot, finely chopped
1 celery stick, finely chopped
1 onion, chopped
2 garlic cloves, chopped
1 teaspoon ground cumin
1 teaspoon ground coriander
½ teaspoon ground cinnamon
½ teaspoon dried chilli flakes
400 g (13 oz) can kidney beans
100 g (3½ oz) frozen peas
400 g (13 oz) can tomatoes
2 tablespoons tomato purée
250 ml (8 fl oz) lager-style beer
  or vegetable stock
salt and pepper
2 tablespoons chopped coriander,
  to garnish
soft flour tortillas and grated
  Cheddar cheese, to serve

- Heat the oil in a large saucepan or casserole and add the carrots, celery, onion and garlic. Cook for 8 minutes, until beginning to soften.

- Stir in the ground spices and chilli flakes, and cook for a further minute, stirring constantly. Drain and rinse the kidney beans, then put in the pan along with all the remaining ingredients and bring to the boil. Reduce the heat, cover and simmer gently for 15–20 minutes, until thickened and tender. Season to taste, scatter with chopped coriander and serve with warmed soft tortillas and grated Cheddar.

10 Chilli Bean Tortillas

Heat 2 tablespoons olive or vegetable oil in a large frying pan, and cook 1 finely chopped onion, 1 chopped red pepper and 2 chopped garlic cloves for 4–5 minutes, until lightly coloured. Add 1 teaspoon ground cumin, 1 teaspoon ground coriander and ½ teaspoon each ground cinnamon and dried chilli flakes, and cook for 1 minute, then pour in a 300 g (10 oz) jar spicy tomato salsa and 400 g (13 oz) can kidney beans, drained and rinsed. Simmer gently for 2–3 minutes. Meanwhile, heat 1 tablespoon oil in a large frying pan and fry 4 large eggs for 2–3 minutes, until the white is set and the yolk still runny. Toast 4 large soft flour tortillas and place 1 on each of 4 serving plates. Spoon over the spicy beans and top each one with a fried egg. Serve immediately.

20 Cheat's Veggie Chilli

Cook the onion, red pepper and garlic following the 10-minute recipe. Stir in a 30 g (1¼ oz) sachet chilli con carne seasoning mix, 100 g (3½ oz) frozen peas, 400 g (13 oz) can kidney beans, drained and rinsed, 400 g (13 oz) can tomatoes, 2 tablespoons tomato purée and 100 ml (3½ fl oz) lager or vegetable stock. Simmer for 10–15 minutes. Serve with 4 warmed flour tortillas, grated cheese and chopped coriander.

Basil and Rocket Pesto with Wholewheat Spaghetti

Serves 4

50 g (2 oz) sunflower or pumpkin seeds
500 g (1 lb) wholewheat spaghetti
1 small garlic clove, roughly chopped
1 small bunch of basil
75 g (3 oz) rocket leaves
25 g (1 oz) Parmesan-style cheese, finely grated, plus extra to serve (optional)
6 tablespoons olive oil
1 tablespoon lemon juice
coarse sea salt and pepper

- Place the seeds in a small, dry frying pan and toast gently for 3–4 minutes, shaking the pan frequently, until lightly toasted and golden. Tip on to a plate to cool.

- Cook the spaghetti in a large saucepan of lightly salted boiling water for 11–12 minutes, or according to packet instructions, until al dente.

- Meanwhile, crush the garlic together with a generous pinch of sea salt using a pestle and mortar. Add the basil and rocket leaves, and pound until crushed to a coarse paste.

- Add the toasted seeds and pound to a paste, then transfer to a bowl and stir in the cheese, olive oil and lemon juice. Season to taste with plenty of black pepper and more salt, if necessary.

- Drain the pasta and toss immediately with the pesto. Divide between 4 shallow bowls and serve with extra cheese, if desired.

Quick Basil and Rocket Pesto

Cook 500 g (1 lb) quick-cook pasta according to packet instructions. Place 50 g (2 oz) toasted sunflower or pumpkin seeds in a mini-chopper or the small bowl of a food processor with 1 roughly chopped clove of garlic, 1 bunch of basil and 75 g (3 oz) rocket leaves. Season, pulse until finely chopped, then transfer to a bowl and stir in 25 g (1 oz) grated Parmesan-style cheese, 6 tablespoons olive oil and 1 tablespoon lemon juice. Drain the pasta, toss with the pesto and serve immediately.

Creamy Gnocchi Pesto Bake Cook 500 g (1 lb) ready-made gnocchi in a large saucepan of lightly salted boiling water for about 2 minutes, or according to packet instructions, until just tender. Meanwhile, make the pesto following the 10-minute recipe, then stir in 300 ml (½ pint) crème fraîche. Stir in the cooked gnocchi, then transfer to a large ovenproof dish and sprinkle with 2 tablespoons grated Parmesan-style cheese. Cook in a preheated oven, 190 °C (375 °F), Gas Mark 5, for about 20 minutes until bubbling and golden. Serve with extra rocket leaves, if desired.

BUD-VEGG-KIZ

Mustardy Squash, Carrot and Sweet Potato Casserole

Serves 4

3 tablespoons vegetable oil

1 red onion, roughly chopped

4 garlic cloves, chopped

750 g (1½ lb) butternut squash, peeled, deseeded and cut into bite-sized chunks

500 g (1 lb) sweet potatoes, peeled and cut into bite-sized chunks

2 carrots, peeled and cut into bite-sized chunks

125 ml (4 fl oz) dry white wine

1 teaspoon dried tarragon or rosemary

400 ml (14 fl oz) hot vegetable stock

2 tablespoons wholegrain mustard

200 g (7 oz) spinach, chopped

salt and pepper

steamed rice, to serve

- Heat the oil in a heavy-based saucepan or casserole. Cook the onion and garlic for 3–4 minutes, until softened. Add the squash, sweet potato and carrot, and cook for a further 3–4 minutes, until lightly golden.

- Pour in the wine and herbs and reduce by half. Add the vegetable stock and mustard to the pan, then season generously, bring to the boil and simmer gently for about 15 minutes, until the vegetables are tender.

- Stir in the spinach and cook until wilted, then serve in bowls with steamed couscous or rice.

Mustardy Carrot Salad Peel and grate 4 carrots and place in a large bowl with ½ red onion, finely chopped, and 100 g (3½ oz) baby spinach leaves. Combine 3 tablespoons olive or vegetable oil in a small bowl with 1 tablespoon mustard, 1 small crushed garlic clove, 1 teaspoon freshly chopped tarragon or rosemary and 2 teaspoons white wine vinegar. Whisk to combine, and season to taste. Toss with the carrot salad and serve immediately.

Mustardy Squash and Sweet Potato Mash Cook 750 g (1½ lb) butternut squash, peeled, deseeded and cut into bite-sized chunks, 500 g (1 lb) peeled and cubed sweet potatoes and 4 whole garlic cloves in a large saucepan of lightly salted boiling water or vegetable stock for about 15 minutes, until just tender. Drain and return to the pan with 50 g (2 oz) butter, 2 tablespoons wholegrain mustard and 2 tablespoons freshly chopped parsley, if desired. Mash until almost smooth, then season to taste with salt and pepper. Serve the mustardy mash with wilted spinach leaves and grilled veggie sausages.

Aloo Tikki with Coriander and Mint Chutney

Serves 4

750 g (1½ lb) potatoes, peeled and cut into chunks

4 tablespoons chopped fresh coriander

2 teaspoons finely grated fresh root ginger

2½ teaspoons garam masala

1 green chilli, chopped and deseeded

75 g (3 oz) frozen peas, defrosted

100 g (3½ oz) frozen spinach, defrosted

2 tablespoons chopped mint

200 ml (7 fl oz) plain yogurt

2 teaspoons lemon juice

75 g (3 oz) fresh breadcrumbs

2–3 tablespoons plain flour

vegetable oil, for shallow frying

salt and pepper

- Cook the potatoes in a large saucepan of lightly salted boiling water for about 10 minutes or until just tender. Drain well.

- Meanwhile, mix half the coriander with the grated ginger, garam masala, chopped chilli and peas. Place the spinach in the middle of a clean tea towel, bring up the edges and twist the spinach in the tea towel over a sink to squeeze out the excess moisture. Add to the bowl of spices, season generously with salt and pepper and mix well to combine. Set aside.

- To make the chutney, mix the remaining coriander with the mint, yogurt and lemon juice, season to taste and set aside.

- Add the potatoes to the spinach and peas, and mash well to combine. Add the breadcrumbs and mix thoroughly to form a soft dough mixture. Form into 20–24 small patties and dust in the flour.

- Heat the oil in a large frying pan and shallow fry the patties for 3–4 minutes, turning once, until crisp and golden. Drain on kitchen paper and serve with the chutney.

---

10 Stuffed Naan with Coriander and Mint Chutney Heat 2 tablespoons oil in a large nonstick frying pan, and cook 2 teaspoons finely grated fresh root ginger, 1 chopped and deseeded green chilli and 2 crushed garlic cloves gently for 1–2 minutes, until lightly golden. Wash, trim and roughly chop 250 g (8 oz) spinach and add to the pan with 200 g (7 oz) frozen peas, 2½ teaspoons garam masala, 2 tablespoons lemon juice and 2 tablespoons chopped fresh

coriander. Season generously and cook for 3–4 minutes, until the peas are just tender and the spinach wilted. Make the chutney following the main recipe. Split open 4 large naan breads and spoon the spiced pea and spinach mixture into the naans. Serve with the coriander and mint chutney.

20 Potato and Spinach Curry with Coriander Cook the ginger, chilli and garlic following the 10-minute recipe. Add 750 g (1½ lb) peeled potatoes, cut into small chunks, 2½ teaspoons garam masala and 2 tablespoons medium curry paste, and cook for 2 minutes. Add 4 diced tomatoes and 350 ml (12 fl oz) hot vegetable stock, then cover and simmer for 12 minutes. Add 250 g (8 oz) spinach and cook for 1–2 minutes. Serve topped with natural yogurt and chopped coriander.

BUD-VEGG-HYM

Feta, Spring Onion and Walnut Tartlets

Serves 4

4 slices of brown bread, crusts removed

150 g (5 oz) feta cheese, crumbled

2 spring onions, thinly sliced

25 g (1 oz) walnut pieces, lightly crushed

8 cherry tomatoes, cut into quarters

1 tablespoon olive oil

salt and pepper

To serve

200 g (7 oz) mixed salad leaves

½ cucumber, sliced

- Preheat the oven to 200°C (400°F), Gas Mark 6. Use a rolling pin to roll the bread out thinly. Cut each slice into a circle, approximately 12 cm (5 inches) in diameter, and press the circles into 4 large nonstick muffin or Yorkshire pudding tins. Cook in the preheated oven for 7–8 minutes, until crisp and golden.

- Meanwhile, mix the crumbled feta with the spring onions, walnut pieces and tomatoes. Season to taste, then spoon the mixture into the toasted tart cases. Drizzle with the olive oil and serve with a mixed leaf and cucumber salad.

2 Feta, Spring Onion and Walnut Pasta

Salad Cook 400 g (13 oz) wholewheat penne in a large saucepan of lightly salted boiling water for 11–12 minutes, or according to packet instructions, until al dente. Meanwhile, place 200 g (7 oz) crumbled feta in a large bowl with 4 thinly sliced spring onions, 50 g (2 oz) walnut pieces and 12 quartered cherry tomatoes. Drain the pasta and refresh under cold running water. Drain well and tip into the bowl with 2 tablespoons lemon juice, 2 tablespoons olive oil and plenty of black pepper. Toss to combine and heap into bowls to serve.

3 Feta, Spring Onion and Walnut Tart

Roll 500 g (1 lb) ready-made puff pastry into a rectangle measuring approximately 30 x 20 cm (12 x 8 inches). Place on a lightly greased baking sheet and score a border about 1.5 cm (¾ inch) in from the edges all the way around the pastry, not quite cutting through. Scatter 200 g (7 oz) crumbled feta, 4 thinly sliced spring onions, 50 g (2 oz) walnut pieces and 12 quartered cherry tomatoes over the pastry, keeping within the border. Drizzle with 1 tablespoon olive oil and cook in a preheated oven, 200°C (400°F), Gas Mark 6, for about 20 minutes until crisp and golden. Serve with salad.

Tomato and Mascarpone Penne Pasta

Serves 4

500 g (1 lb) passata
1 garlic clove, crushed
2 tablespoons olive oil
½ teaspoon sugar
1 teaspoon dried oregano
1 teaspoon finely grated lemon rind (optional)
400 g (13 oz) penne pasta
150 g (5 oz) mascarpone or cream cheese
salt and pepper

- Pour the passata into a saucepan with the garlic, olive oil, sugar, oregano and lemon rind, if using. Cover loosely with a lid, bring to the boil, then simmer gently for 15 minutes.

- Meanwhile, cook the pasta in a large saucepan of lightly salted boiling water for 11 minutes, or according to packet instructions, until al dente. Drain and return to the pan.

- Stir the mascarpone into the pasta sauce, season lightly with salt and pepper, then pour over the pasta. Stir briefly to combine and serve immediately in shallow bowls.

Quick Tomato and Mascarpone Pasta

Sauce Cook 400 g (13 oz) quick-cook pasta shapes in a saucepan of lightly salted boiling water for 3–5 minutes, or according to packet instructions, until al dente. Meanwhile, warm through 450 g (14½ oz) ready-made tomato pasta sauce. Stir 150 g (5 oz) mascarpone or cream cheese into the sauce, with 1 small bunch of chopped basil, if desired. Serve hot with the drained pasta.

Tomato and Mascarpone Bake

Cook 350 g (11½ oz) quick-cook pasta shapes in a saucepan of lightly salted boiling water for 3 minutes, or according to packet instructions, until almost al dente. Meanwhile, combine 500 g (1 lb) passata, 1 crushed garlic clove, 2 tablespoons olive oil, ½ teaspoon sugar, 1 teaspoon dried oregano and 1 teaspoon finely grated lemon rind, if using, in a large pan, and place over a medium heat until simmering gently. Drain the pasta and stir into the sauce. Tip into a large ovenproof dish and scatter with 150 g (5 oz) grated Cheddar cheese. Cook in a preheated oven, 200°C (400°F), Gas Mark 6, for 20–25 minutes until bubbling and golden. Spoon into dishes and serve with extra cheese, if desired.

 # Brie and Thyme Melts

Serves 4

1 ciabatta-style loaf, cut in half
   horizontally
6 tablespoons onion or
   caramelized onion chutney
200 g (7 oz) Brie or Camembert
   cheese, sliced
1 teaspoon dried thyme
4 teaspoons chilli, garlic or basil oil
tomato salad, to serve (optional)

- Cut the two pieces of bread in half to give 4 portions. Arrange, cut side up, on a baking sheet and spread each piece with the onion chutney.

- Lay the Brie slices on top and sprinkle with the thyme. Drizzle with the flavoured oil and cook under a preheated grill for 3–4 minutes, until the cheese begins to melt. Serve immediately with a tomato salad, if desired.

 Whole Baked Cheese with Garlic and Thyme Cut some little slits in the top of a whole 250 g (8 oz) round Camembert or Brie. Insert 1 thinly sliced garlic clove and 5–6 little thyme sprigs into the slits. Drizzle with 2 teaspoons chilli, garlic or basil oil, then wrap in a loose foil parcel and cook in a preheated oven, 180°C (350°F), Gas Mark 4, for about 15 minutes until soft and oozing. Serve with toasted ciabatta, onion chutney and a tomato salad.

Brie, Thyme and Onion Pizza Place 375 g (12 oz) ready-rolled shortcrust pastry on a large greased baking sheet and fold in the edges by about 1 cm (½ inch) to create a crust. Spread with 6 tablespoons onion chutney, then top with 200 g (7 oz) sliced Brie or Camembert cheese. Sprinkle 1 teaspoon dried thyme over the cheese and drizzle with 4 teaspoons chilli, garlic or basil oil. Cook in a preheated oven, 200°C (400°F), Gas Mark 6, for about 20 minutes until the pastry is crisp and golden and the cheese has melted. Serve with a tomato salad.

30 Bean Burgers with Garlicky Yogurt

Serves 4

3 tablespoons vegetable oil
1 onion, finely chopped
1 garlic clove, chopped
400 g (13 oz) can kidney beans,
    drained and rinsed
400 g (13 oz) can black-eyed
    beans, drained and rinsed
1 tablespoon tomato purée
1 teaspoon paprika (optional)
4 tablespoons finely chopped
    flat leaf parsley
1 small egg, lightly beaten
100 g (3½ oz) fresh white
    breadcrumbs
250 ml (8 fl oz) natural yogurt
1 small garlic clove, crushed
2 teaspoons lemon juice
salt and pepper
4 soft flour tortillas, warmed,
    to serve
lettuce leaves, to garnish

- Heat 2 tablespoons of the oil in a small frying pan and cook the onion gently for 6–7 minutes. Add the chopped garlic and cook for a further 2–3 minutes, until really soft and golden.

- Meanwhile, place both lots of beans in the large bowl of a food processor with the tomato purée, paprika, if using, and half the parsley. Pulse until the mixture becomes a coarse paste. Tip into a bowl and add the egg, breadcrumbs and cooked onion mixture. Season with salt and pepper, then mix well and shape into 4 large burgers.

- Heat the remaining oil in a large nonstick frying pan and fry the burgers gently for 8–10 minutes, turning once, until crisp and golden.

- Meanwhile, mix the yogurt with the crushed garlic, the remaining parsley and the lemon juice. Season with salt and pepper and set aside.

- Serve the burgers with warmed tortillas and the yogurt and garnish with lettuce leaves.

 Mixed Bean Hummus Place a 400 g (13 oz) can drained mixed beans in a food processor with 1 tablespoon tomato purée, 1 teaspoon paprika, 4 tablespoons finely chopped flat leaf parsley, 1 small crushed garlic clove and 2 teaspoons lemon juice, and blend to a paste. Add enough yogurt to give a smooth, creamy consistency, then season to taste and serve with a selection of raw vegetables for dipping.

Mixed Bean Tortilla Parcels Make Mixed Bean Hummus, following the 10-minute recipe. Divide the hummus between 4 large soft flour tortillas, and top with 1 sliced red pepper, 1 thinly sliced celery stick, ½ a thinly sliced red onion and 100 g (3½ oz) grated Cheddar cheese. Fold the sides of the tortillas over to form 4 neat parcels and toast on a preheated hot griddle pan for about 8 minutes, turning once, until hot and lightly charred. Serve immediately with shredded iceberg lettuce and tzatziki or salsa, if desired.

Baked Peppers with Feta and Spring Onion

Serves 4

4 red or yellow peppers

4 small tomatoes, halved

200 g (7 oz) feta cheese, sliced

3 spring onions, finely sliced

2 tablespoons olive or vegetable oil, plus extra for greasing

250 g (8 oz) couscous

25 g (1 oz) butter

300 ml (½ pint) boiling vegetable stock or water

freshly ground black pepper

2 tablespoons pumpkin or sunflower seeds, to garnish (optional)

- Preheat the oven to 200°C (400°F), Gas Mark 6, and lightly grease a baking sheet. Cut the peppers in half lengthways and remove the seeds and cores. Place all 8 halves on the baking sheet and fill with the tomato halves, the slices of feta and spring onions. Season with black pepper, drizzle with the oil and cook in the preheated oven for 20–25 minutes, until softened and golden.

- Meanwhile, put the couscous into a bowl with the butter and pour over the boiling stock. Cover and set aside for 5–8 minutes, until the liquid has been absorbed and the grains are tender.

- Serve the baked peppers with the couscous, scattered with pumpkin or sunflower seeds, if using.

---

1 **Pepper, Feta and Spring Onion Salad**
Drain a 450 g (14½ oz) can whole roasted red peppers, then cut in half lengthways and remove any seeds. Slice the flesh into strips and toss gently with 200 g (7 oz) sliced feta cheese and 3 finely sliced spring onions. Cut 4 small tomatoes into wedges. Spoon 500 g (1 lb) ready-made couscous salad on to 4 plates and scatter over the tomato wedges and red pepper mixture. Sprinkle with 2 tablespoons pumpkin or sunflower seeds to serve.

2 **Pepper, Feta and Spring Onion Tabbouleh** Put 250 g (8 oz) couscous into a bowl with 25 g (1 oz) butter and pour over 300 ml (½ pint) boiling vegetable stock or water. Cover and set aside for 5–8 minutes, until the liquid has been absorbed and the grains are tender. Use a fork to fluff up the grains, and spread over a large baking sheet to cool. Meanwhile, finely dice 1 red pepper and 1 yellow pepper, then deseed and finely dice 2 ripe but firm tomatoes. Thinly slice 4 spring onions and finely chop

1 large bunch of flat leaf parsley. Fold all the ingredients into the cooled couscous with 2 tablespoons each of lemon juice and olive oil. Spoon into shallow dishes and crumble 200 g (7 oz) feta cheese over the top. Serve scattered with the 2 tablespoons pumpkin or sunflower seeds, if using.

Marinated Tofu with Vegetables

Serves 4

3 tablespoons ketjap manis
or sweet soy sauce

1 teaspoon crushed garlic

2 teaspoons minced ginger

2 tablespoons sweet chilli
dipping sauce

500 g (1 lb) firm tofu, cut into
1.5-cm (¾-inch) slices

2 tablespoons vegetable or
groundnut oil

1 carrot, peeled and cut into
fine matchsticks

500 g (1 lb) pak choi, sliced

200 g (7 oz) bean sprouts

225 g (7½ oz) can bamboo
shoots in water

6 tablespoons oyster sauce

2 teaspoons golden sesame
seeds, to garnish (optional)

- Mix the ketjap manis, garlic, ginger and sweet chilli dipping sauce in a small bowl. Arrange the tofu slices in a shallow dish and pour over the marinade, turning to coat. Set aside to marinate for about 20 minutes.

- Carefully transfer the tofu slices to a foil-lined grill rack, reserving the marinade. Cook under a preheated grill for about 3 minutes on each side, until golden. Remove from the heat and keep warm.

- Meanwhile, heat the oil in a wok over a moderate heat. Stir-fry the carrot and pak choi for 4–5 minutes, until beginning to soften. Add the bean sprouts and bamboo shoots and cook for 1 minute, then pour in the remaining marinade and the oyster sauce.

- Spoon the vegetables into deep bowls, top with the grilled tofu slices and sprinkle with golden sesame seeds, if using.

Marinated Tofu Stir-Fry

Heat 2 tablespoons vegetable or groundnut oil in a wok and stir-fry 625 g (1¼ lb) ready-prepared mixed stir-fry vegetables for 4–5 minutes, until beginning to soften. Pour in 250 g (8 oz) ready-made oyster and spring onion stir-fry sauce and cook until hot. Divide between 4 deep bowls, then top with 150 g (5 oz) ready-prepared marinated tofu strips. Serve sprinkled with sesame seeds, if using.

Tofu and Vegetable Noodles

Cook the stir-fried vegetables following the main recipe, adding 150 g (5 oz) ready-prepared marinated tofu strips or cubed firm tofu, along with the bean sprouts and bamboo shoots. Meanwhile, cook 250 g (8 oz) medium dried egg noodles according to packet instructions, then drain and toss with the vegetables and tofu. Serve with soy sauce.

 # Roasted Butternut Couscous with Crumbly Cheese

Serves 4

1 kg (2 lb) butternut squash, peeled and cut into bite-sized pieces

3 tablespoons olive or vegetable oil

1 teaspoon chilli flakes

1 teaspoon fennel seeds

250 g (8 oz) couscous

300 ml (½ pint) boiling vegetable stock or water

200 g (7 oz) Wensleydale, Cheshire or similar crumbly white cheese

2 spring onions, finely sliced

2 tablespoons toasted pine nuts (optional)

salt and pepper

- Preheat the oven to 220°C (425°F), Gas Mark 7. Parboil the squash in a large saucepan of lightly salted water for 5–7 minutes. Drain really well and tip into a roasting tin. Drizzle with 2 tablespoons of the oil, sprinkle with the chilli flakes and fennel seeds, then season generously with salt and pepper. Cook in the preheated oven for 18–20 minutes, until tender.

- Meanwhile, place the couscous in a large bowl. Stir in the remaining oil and a generous pinch of salt. Add the boiling stock, then cover and set aside for 5–10 minutes, until the grains are tender and all the liquid has been absorbed.

- Spoon the couscous on to 4 plates, scatter with the roasted butternut squash and crumble the cheese on top. Sprinkle over the spring onions and pine nuts, if using, and serve immediately.

---

1 Roasted-Style Couscous with Crumbly Cheese Heat 3 tablespoons oil in a frying pan and fry 250 g (8 oz) couscous for 1–2 minutes, stirring constantly. Add 2 sliced spring onions and 1 teaspoon chilli flakes. Season and fry for a further minute. Pour in 300 ml (½ pint) hot vegetable stock, remove from the heat and cover tightly for 5–6 minutes, until the grains are tender and the liquid has been absorbed. Spoon into bowls, crumble over 200 g (7 oz) Wensleydale and scatter with 2 tablespoons toasted pine nuts, if desired.

2 Root Vegetable Couscous with Parmesan Cheese Cook 450 g (14½ oz) each of carrots and parsnips, peeled and cut into chunks, in a large saucepan of lightly salted boiling water for 10–12 minutes, until tender. Heat 2 tablespoons olive oil in a large nonstick frying pan, and fry the carrots and parsnips with 1 teaspoon chilli flakes and 1 teaspoon fennel seeds over a high heat for 5–6 minutes, until lightly golden. Season to taste. Meanwhile, follow the main recipe to cook 250 g (8 oz) couscous. Spoon the vegetables over the couscous, and serve topped with 50 g (2 oz) grated Parmesan-style cheese.

 # Spicy Kidney Beans with Rice

Serves 4

250 g (8 oz) long-grain rice

2 tablespoons olive or vegetable oil

1 large red onion, chopped

1 red pepper, cored, deseeded and chopped

2 celery sticks, chopped

2 teaspoons Cajun- or Mexican-style spice blend

2 x 400 g (13 oz) cans red kidney beans, drained and rinsed

3 ripe tomatoes, diced

1 tablespoon red wine vinegar

1 teaspoon Tabasco sauce, plus extra to serve

125 ml (4 fl oz) water

salt and pepper

2 tablespoons chopped chives, to garnish (optional)

4 tablespoons crème fraîche, to serve (optional)

- Bring a large pan of lightly salted water to the boil and cook the rice for 12 minutes, or according to packet instructions, until just tender. Drain and keep hot.

- Meanwhile, heat the oil in a large, deep-sided frying pan and add the onion, pepper and celery. Cook for 8–9 minutes, until softened. Add the spice mix, cook for 1 minute, then stir in the kidney beans, tomatoes, vinegar, Tabasco and measured water.

- Cover and simmer gently for 7–8 minutes, adding a little more water if necessary. Season to taste and scatter with the chopped chives, if using. Serve with the tender rice, extra Tabasco and crème fraîche, if desired.

Spicy Mexican Rice Salad Finely chop 1 red pepper and mix with ½ a finely chopped red onion and 2 finely chopped celery sticks. Stir in 250 g (8 oz) cooked wild and basmati rice and 400 g (13 oz) can of kidney beans, rinsed and drained. Add 2 deseeded and chopped tomatoes, 2 tablespoons chopped chives and 2 tablespoons lime juice. Season generously and serve with lightly salted tortilla chips.

One-Pot Spicy Mexican Rice Heat 2 tablespoons olive or vegetable oil in a large saucepan or casserole, and cook 1 chopped red onion, 1 chopped red pepper and 2 chopped celery sticks over a medium-high heat for about 5 minutes, until slightly coloured. Stir in 250 g (8 oz) rinsed long-grain rice and 2 teaspoons Mexican-style spice mix and cook for 1 minute, then add 1 tablespoon tomato purée, 400 g (13 oz) can of chopped tomatoes, 400 g (13 oz) can of drained kidney beans and 600 ml (1 pint) boiling vegetable stock. Reduce the heat, cover with a tight-fitting lid and simmer gently for 20–23 minutes, until the rice is tender and the liquid has been absorbed. Serve with Tabasco and soured cream, and scatter with chopped chives, if desired.

 Potato and Onion Pizza

Serves 4

300 g (10 oz) plain flour
1 sachet of fast-action dried yeast
1½ teaspoons caster sugar
1 teaspoon salt
175 ml (6 fl oz) warm water
3 tablespoons olive oil, plus extra
   for greasing
125 ml (4 fl oz) crème fraîche
200 g (7 oz) unpeeled new
   potatoes, very thinly sliced
   on a mandolin
½ onion, very thinly sliced
   on a mandolin
2 teaspoons dried thyme
100 g (3½ oz) Emmental or
   Cheddar cheese, grated
12 black olives (optional)
cracked black pepper

- Preheat the oven to 200°C (400°F), Gas Mark 6, and lightly grease a baking sheet. In a large bowl, mix together the flour, yeast, sugar and salt. Make a well in the centre and pour in the warm water and 2 tablespoons of the oil. Combine to make a soft dough, then roll out to a rectangle about 35 x 25 cm (14 x 10 inches). Transfer to the baking sheet and cook in the preheated oven for 5 minutes or until just beginning to colour.

- Spoon 4 tablespoons of the crème fraîche over the pizza base. Top with the slices of potato and onion, then sprinkle over the thyme and scatter with the cheese. Drizzle the remaining oil over the pizza and return to the oven. Increase the temperature to 220°C (425°F), Gas Mark 7, and bake for about 15 minutes, until golden.

- Cut the pizza into slices, scatter with the olives, if desired, and top with the remaining crème fraîche. Season with cracked black pepper and serve hot.

---

1 **Creamy Potato and Onion Gnocchi**

Heat 2 tablespoons olive oil in a frying pan, and cook 1 chopped onion and 2 chopped garlic cloves for 7–8 minutes. Meanwhile, cook 500 g (1 lb) ready-made gnocchi according to packet instructions. Add 400 ml (14 fl oz) crème fraîche, 1 teaspoon thyme leaves and 150 g (5 oz) grated Emmental or Cheddar cheese to the onion, and stir for 1 minute. Season generously and stir in the drained gnocchi. Spoon into 4 bowls and serve immediately, with extra cheese, if desired.

---

2 **Potato and Onion Gratin** Cook 1 kg (2 lb) thinly sliced potatoes in a large saucepan of lightly salted boiling water for 8–10 minutes, until just tender. Drain well and tip into a large, heat-resistant bowl. Meanwhile, heat 2 tablespoons of olive oil in a frying pan, and fry 1 thinly sliced onion and 2 chopped garlic cloves for 6–7 minutes, until lightly golden. Stir in 500 ml (17 fl oz) crème fraîche, 1 teaspoon dried thyme and plenty of salt and pepper. Bring to the boil, then remove from the heat. Pour the sauce over the potatoes, shaking gently to combine, then tip into a large ovenproof dish. Sprinkle with 150 g (5 oz) grated Emmental or Cheddar cheese and cook under a moderate grill for 6–8 minutes, until bubbling and golden. Serve with green salad, scattered with 12 black olives, if desired.

 # Lentil Bolognese

Serves 4

1 onion, roughly chopped
1 carrot, peeled and chopped
1 celery stick, roughly chopped
1 garlic clove, peeled
3 tablespoons olive oil
125 ml (4 fl oz) red wine
100 ml (3½ fl oz) water
75 g (3 oz) tomato purée
400 g (13 oz) can chopped
   tomatoes
1 teaspoon dried mixed herbs
2 x 400 g (13 oz) cans green
   lentils, drained and rinsed
salt and pepper

To serve

50 g (2 oz) grated Parmesan-
   style cheese
crusty bread

- Place the onion, carrot, celery and garlic in a food processor and pulse briefly until finely chopped. Heat the olive oil in a large, heavy-based casserole or saucepan. Add the vegetable mixture and cook for 5–6 minutes, stirring frequently, until softened and lightly golden.

- Pour in the red wine, measured water, tomato purée, chopped tomatoes and herbs, and season to taste with salt and pepper. Simmer gently for about 15 minutes, then add the lentils and simmer for a further 5–7 minutes, until thickened and tender. Spoon into deep bowls, sprinkle with cheese and serve with plenty of fresh, crusty bread.

1 Cheat's Lentil Bolognese

Place 1 roughly chopped onion, 1 peeled and roughly chopped carrot, 1 roughly chopped celery stick and 1 garlic clove in a food processor and pulse until finely chopped. Heat 3 tablespoons olive oil in a large, heavy-based casserole or saucepan and cook the vegetable mixture for 5–6 minutes, stirring frequently, until softened and lightly golden. Stir in a 500 g (1 lb) jar tomato pasta sauce and 2 x 400 g (13 oz) cans green lentils in water, drained and rinsed. Simmer gently for 2–3 minutes, then serve as above, with Parmesan-style cheese and crusty bread.

2 Green Lentil and Vegetable Soup

Cook the vegetables following the 10-minute recipe, then add 400 g (13 oz) can chopped tomatoes, 1 teaspoon dried mixed herbs, 2 x 400 g (13 oz) cans green lentils in water, drained and rinsed, and 1 litre (1¾ pints) hot vegetable stock. Season well, bring to the boil and simmer for 12–15 minutes, until tender. Use a hand-held blender to blend until smooth, then ladle the soup into bowls and serve with 50 g (2 oz) grated Parmesan-style cheese.

 # Homemade Baked Beans

Serves 4

2 tablespoons olive or
  vegetable oil
1 onion, thinly sliced
2 garlic cloves, crushed
500 g (1 lb) passata
100 ml (3½ fl oz) hot vegetable
  stock or water
½ teaspoon sugar
2 x 400 g (13 oz) cans haricot
  beans, drained and rinsed
pinch of cayenne (optional)
pinch of cinnamon (optional)
salt and pepper
4 thick slices of granary bread,
  to serve

- Heat the olive oil in a heavy-based saucepan and cook the onion gently for 3–4 minutes. Add the garlic and cook for a further 2 minutes, until softened and golden.

- Add the passata, stock, sugar, beans and spices, if using, and season to taste with salt and pepper. Simmer gently for 12–14 minutes, until rich and thick.

- Meanwhile, toast the bread until golden and place on 4 plates. Serve the beans spooned over the toast.

Crunchy Bean Salad
Place 2 x 400 g (13 oz) cans haricot beans, drained and rinsed, in a bowl and add 3 diced tomatoes, 1 crushed garlic clove, 1 finely chopped red onion, 3 tablespoons oil, a pinch of sugar and 1 tablespoon red wine vinegar. Stir to combine, then spoon into bowls and serve scattered with 100 g (3½ oz) ready-made croûtons.

 Crispy-Topped Baked Beans
Make the baked beans following the main recipe, adding an extra 50 ml (2 fl oz) vegetable stock or water. Meanwhile, melt 25 g (1 oz) butter in a large frying pan with 150 g (5 oz) fresh breadcrumbs. Stir over a low heat for 5–6 minutes, until beginning to crisp, then tip into a bowl with 2 tablespoons chopped parsley and 2 tablespoons grated Parmesan-style cheese. Transfer the beans into a large ovenproof dish and sprinkle over the breadcrumb topping. Cook in a preheated oven, 200°C (400°F), Gas Mark 6, for about 10 minutes, until the topping is crisp and lightly golden. Serve with green salad.

30 Chunky Vegetable and Cheese Gratin

Serves 4

100 g (3½ oz) butter

1 kg (2 lb) mixed vegetables (courgettes, carrots, leeks, mushrooms), cut into bite-sized pieces

500 g (1 lb) potatoes, peeled and cut into chunks

50 g (2 oz) plain flour

575 ml (18 fl oz) milk

2 teaspoons Dijon mustard (optional)

200 g (7 oz) mature Cheddar or Double Gloucester cheese, grated

salt and pepper

- Melt half the butter in a large, heavy-based casserole or saucepan and gently cook the mixed vegetables for about 20 minutes, stirring occasionally, until tender and golden.

- Cook the potatoes in a large saucepan of lightly salted boiling water for 10–12 minutes, until just tender.

- Meanwhile, place the remaining butter, the flour and the milk in a saucepan over a medium heat, and stir constantly with a balloon whisk or wooden spoon until thickened. Simmer gently for 1–2 minutes, then stir in the Dijon mustard, if using, and half the grated cheese. Season lightly to taste and set aside.

- Transfer the cooked vegetables to a large ovenproof dish and pour over the cheese sauce. Sprinkle with the remaining cheese and cook under a preheated grill for 5–7 minutes, until bubbling and golden. Serve immediately.

 Quick Vegetable Gratin Melt 50 g (2 oz) butter in a saucepan and cook 1 kg (2 lb) frozen mixed vegetables for 3–4 minutes, stirring occasionally. Meanwhile, make the cheese sauce using 25 g (1 oz) each of flour and butter, and 300 ml (½ pint) milk. Simmer for 1–2 minutes, then stir in 1 teaspoon mustard and 100 g (3½ oz) grated Cheddar cheese. Divide the vegetables between 4 individual ovenproof dishes, then pour over the cheese sauce and cook under a hot grill for 2–3 minutes until just bubbling and golden. Serve with crusty bread and watercress salad.

 Chunky Vegetable Soup with Cheese Croûtons Chop 1 kg (2 lb) mixed vegetables (courgettes, carrots, leeks, mushrooms) finely and cook in 50 g (2 oz) butter with 2 chopped garlic cloves for 7–8 minutes, until lightly golden. Add 1 litre (1¾ pints) hot vegetable stock, season to taste and simmer for 7–8 minutes, until tender. Meanwhile, scatter 100 g (3½ oz) of grated Cheddar or Double Gloucester cheese on 8 slices of granary baguette and cook under the grill for 4–5 minutes, until melted and lightly golden. Use a slotted spoon to remove half the vegetables from the pan and set aside. Use a hand-held blender to blend the remaining soup, then return the vegetables to the pan and ladle the soup into 4 bowls. Top with the cheesy croûtons and serve.

BUD-VEGG-QOJ

Vegetable Noodles with Stir-Fry Sauce

Serves 4

400 g (13 oz) medium dried egg noodles

2 tablespoons vegetable oil

2 carrots, peeled and cut into thin batons

250 g (8 oz) broccoli, cut into small florets

4 spring onions, cut into 1.5-cm (¾-inch) lengths

300 g (10 oz) Chinese-style stir-fry sauce

150 g (5 oz) bean sprouts

2 tablespoons roasted cashew nuts, crushed, to garnish (optional)

- Bring a large saucepan of water to the boil, add the egg noodles and immediately remove from the heat. Cover and set aside for 4–5 minutes, until tender. Alternatively, cook according to packet instructions. Drain and refresh under cold running water.

- Meanwhile, heat the oil in a wok, and add the carrots, broccoli and spring onions. Stir-fry gently for 4–5 minutes, until starting to soften.

- Add the stir-fry sauce and heat until bubbling, then add the bean sprouts and drained noodles. Toss until heated through, then serve in 4 large bowls, sprinkled with crushed cashew nuts, if using.

Quick Noodle Salad Cook 400 g (13 oz) medium dried egg noodles following the main recipe. Peel 2 carrots and cut into thin batons and thinly slice 4 spring onions, then toss the vegetables with the cooled drained noodles and 150 g (5 oz) bean sprouts. Make a dressing by combining 2 tablespoons Chinese-style stir-fry sauce, 1 tablespoon light soy sauce and 3 tablespoons vegetable oil. Toss into the noodles, then heap into 4 bowls and serve scattered with 2 tablespoons crushed roasted cashews, if desired.

Aromatic Vegetable and Noodle Soup Cook 400 g (13 oz) medium dried egg noodles following the main recipe. Heat 1 tablespoon vegetable oil in a large saucepan, and add 4 spring onions, cut into 1.5-cm (¾-inch) lengths, 1 tablespoon chopped fresh root ginger and 2 sliced garlic cloves. Cook gently for 2 minutes, add 1.2 litres (2 pints) hot vegetable or miso stock, 2 star anise and 3 tablespoons light soy sauce, and bring to the boil. Simmer gently, uncovered, for about 20 minutes to allow the flavours to develop, then stir in 2 carrots, peeled and cut into thin batons, and 250 g (8 oz) small broccoli florets. Cook for 2–3 minutes, until just tender. Stir in 150 g (5 oz) bean sprouts and the noodles for the final minute, then ladle into 4 deep bowls to serve.

QuickCook
Meat and Poultry

Recipes listed by cooking time

3⏱

2⏱

10

30 Farmhouse Meatballs with Couscous

Serves 4

1 onion, roughly chopped

1 celery stick, roughly chopped

100 g (3½ oz) mushrooms

1 large garlic clove, chopped

4 tablespoons olive or
 vegetable oil

500 ml (17 fl oz) boiling ham
 or vegetable stock

400 g (13 oz) can plum tomatoes

250 g (7 oz) couscous

50 g (2 oz) butter

500 g (1 lb) farmhouse or
 Cumberland sausages

2 tablespoons chopped parsley
 (optional)

- Place the onion, celery, mushrooms and garlic in a food processor and pulse until finely chopped. Heat 2 tablespoons of the oil in a large frying pan and cook the chopped vegetables for 8 minutes, until lightly golden and tender. Add 200 ml (7 fl oz) of the stock and the tomatoes to the pan, and simmer gently for about 18 minutes.

- Place the couscous in a bowl with the butter and pour over the remaining stock then cover and set aside for 6–8 minutes, until the grains are tender and all the liquid has been absorbed.

- Meanwhile, remove the skins from the sausages and roll the meat into 16–20 bite-sized meatballs. Heat the remaining oil in a large nonstick frying pan and cook the meatballs for 10–12 minutes, turning frequently, until cooked through.

- Fluff the couscous with a fork, then heap into 4 shallow bowls. Spoon over some sauce and arrange the meatballs on top. Scatter with chopped parsley, if using, and serve immediately.

1○ Quick Sausage and Mushroom Couscous Heat 2 tablespoons oil in a frying pan, and cook 1 chopped onion and 1 chopped garlic clove for 4–5 minutes. Add 100 g (3½ oz) chopped mushrooms and cook for 3 minutes more. Add 225 g (7½ oz) sliced, smoked cooked pork sausage and 350 g (11½ oz) tomato pasta sauce, and bring to the boil. Meanwhile, cook 250 g (8 oz) couscous, following the main recipe. Once the sausage is hot, spoon the sauce over the couscous, scatter with a handful of chopped parsley and serve.

2○ Farmhouse Sausage Stew with Couscous Heat 2 tablespoons olive or vegetable oil in a large, deep-sided frying pan. Fry 8 farmhouse-style sausages over a medium-high heat for 3–4 minutes, until lightly golden. Remove and set aside the sausages and reduce the heat slightly. Add 1 roughly chopped onion and 1 large chopped garlic clove to the pan, and cook for 4–5 minutes, until softened. Add 100 g (3½ oz) roughly chopped mushrooms and cook for 2 minutes, then return the sausages to the pan. Pour in 200 ml (7 fl oz) of boiling ham or vegetable stock, a 400 g (13 oz) can chopped tomatoes and 2 tablespoons sun-dried tomato paste, and simmer for 8–10 minutes, until the sausages are cooked. Cook 250 g (7 oz) couscous, following the main recipe, and serve with the sausages and sauce.

Ginger and Coriander Turkey Burgers

Serves 4

450 g (14½ oz) minced turkey
1 tablespoon finely grated fresh
  root ginger
3 tablespoons finely chopped
  fresh coriander
50 g (2 oz) fresh breadcrumbs
2 teaspoons dark soy sauce
2 tablespoons lightly beaten egg
2 tablespoons vegetable oil
black pepper

To serve

4 tablespoons chilli jam
4 large or 8 small bread rolls, split
  and griddled
4–8 lettuce leaves

- Place the turkey in a large bowl with the ginger, coriander, breadcrumbs and soy sauce. Season with black pepper and add the egg, mixing well to combine. Form into 4 large or 8 small burgers.

- Heat the oil in a large nonstick frying pan and fry the burgers for 3–4 minutes on each side, until cooked through and golden.

- Spread the chilli jam on to the bottom halves of the griddled rolls and top with the lettuce leaves. Place a burger on top of each and cover with the lid. Serve immediately.

---

10 Griddled Turkey with Ginger and Coriander Dressing

Rub 1 tablespoon vegetable oil over 400 g (13 oz) turkey breast steaks. Season with salt and pepper, then heat a griddle pan and cook the turkey steaks for 2–3 minutes on each side, until cooked through and lightly charred. Set aside to cool slightly, then cut into strips. Meanwhile, make a dressing by combining 3 tablespoons vegetable oil with 1 teaspoon grated fresh root ginger, 1 tablespoon chilli jam, 2 teaspoons light soy sauce and 1 tablespoon lime juice. Toss 175 g (6 oz) mixed salad leaves with 3 tablespoons finely chopped fresh coriander, and heap into 4 bowls. Scatter over the turkey strips, then drizzle over the dressing and serve with griddled bread rolls, if desired.

30 Baked Turkey Breast with Ginger and Coriander

Combine 1 tablespoon finely grated fresh root ginger, 3 tablespoons finely chopped fresh coriander, 2 tablespoons chilli jam and 1 tablespoon light soy sauce. Cut some slashes in 4 turkey breast fillet portions, about 150 g (5 oz) each, and massage in the ginger and coriander marinade. Place in an ovenproof dish and cover with foil. Cook in a preheated oven, 200°C (400°F), Gas Mark 6, for about 20 minutes, until cooked through. Serve with 500 g (1 lb) cooked rice, extra chilli jam and lime wedges.

Pork Schnitzel with Feta and Butter Bean Salad

Serves 4

4 boneless pork chops, about 150 g (5 oz) each

2 small eggs, lightly beaten

3 tablespoons seasoned flour

1½ teaspoons dried oregano

grated rind and juice of 1 lemon

100 g (3½ oz) fresh breadcrumbs

4 tablespoons olive or vegetable oil

200 g (7 oz) feta cheese, diced

75 g (3 oz) stoned olives

2 large tomatoes, diced

400 g (13 oz) can butter beans, drained and rinsed

salt and pepper

- Place the pork chops, one at a time, between 2 large pieces of clingfilm and beat with a rolling pin until about 1 cm (½ inch) thick.

- Put the eggs in a large, shallow bowl and place the seasoned flour on a plate. Stir 1 teaspoon of the dried oregano and the lemon rind into the breadcrumbs, season with salt and pepper and scatter on a separate plate.

- Coat the pork chops on both sides in the seasoned flour, followed by the egg and finally the breadcrumb mixture.

- Heat half the oil in a large nonstick frying pan and cook the pork schnitzels for 3–4 minutes on each side, until crispy, golden and cooked through.

- Meanwhile, mix the feta and olives with the diced tomatoes and butter beans. Whisk together the lemon juice, the remaining oil and oregano, and season. Fold into the salad, then spoon on to 4 plates and serve with the pork schnitzel.

---

10 Pork, Feta and Butter Bean Parcels

Heat 4 tablespoons oil in a frying pan and cook 350 g (11½ oz) pork strips for 4–5 minutes. Meanwhile, arrange 4 flour tortillas on 4 warmed plates and top with 75 g (3 oz) salad leaves. Scatter over 400 g (13 oz) can butter beans, drained, rinsed and warmed, 2 large diced tomatoes, 75 g (3 oz) stoned olives, 200 g (7 oz) diced feta cheese and 1 teaspoon dried oregano. Divide the pork between the tortillas and squeeze over some lemon juice. Fold in the sides of the tortillas, then turn to serve.

30 Feta-Stuffed Pork with Butter Beans

Mix 50 g (2 oz) breadcrumbs with 1 deseeded and diced tomato, 25 g (1 oz) stoned olives, 100 g (3½ oz) crumbled feta cheese, the grated rind of 1 lemon and 1½ teaspoons dried oregano. Cut pockets into the sides of 4 thick-cut, boneless pork chops and fill with the prepared mixture. Place on a greased baking sheet, then drizzle with 2 tablespoons of olive oil and the juice of 1 lemon, and roast in a preheated oven, 200°C (400°F), Gas Mark 6,

for 20–25 minutes, until cooked and lightly golden. Meanwhile, warm a rinsed and drained 400 g (13 oz) can butter beans in a pan with 1 deseeded and diced tomato and 50 g (2 oz) stoned olives, then season to taste. Spoon on to 4 plates and serve with the pork chops and their juices.

 # Keema Matar with Mango Chutney

Serves 4

2 tablespoons vegetable oil
1 large onion, chopped
2 garlic cloves, sliced
1.5-cm (¾-inch) piece of fresh root ginger, finely chopped
1 green chilli, deseeded and finely chopped
2.5 cm (1 inch) cinnamon stick
2–3 cardamom pods, crushed
1 teaspoon ground coriander
1 teaspoon ground cumin
½ teaspoon ground turmeric
½ teaspoon garam masala
500 g (1 lb) minced lamb
150 g (5 oz) frozen peas
2 tomatoes, chopped
250 ml (8 fl oz) boiling water
salt and pepper

To serve

4 tablespoons mango chutney
chapattis, naans or boiled rice

- Heat the oil in a large, deep-sided frying pan. Add the onion and cook for 3–4 minutes. Add the garlic, ginger and chilli, and cook for a further 2–3 minutes, until coloured.

- Stir in the spices, then increase the heat and add the minced lamb. Cook for 2–3 minutes, until browned all over.

- Stir in the peas, tomatoes and plenty of seasoning, then pour in the measured boiling water. Bring to the boil, reduce the heat and simmer gently for about 15 minutes, until cooked and thickened. Serve hot with mango chutney, chapattis, naans or boiled rice.

Keema Matar-Style Lamb Chops

Mix 1 teaspoon ground coriander, 1 teaspoon ground cumin, ½ teaspoon ground turmeric, ½ teaspoon garam masala and 1 tablespoon vegetable oil. Rub over 8 lamb chops, about 500 g (1 lb) total weight. Cook on a foil-lined grill rack under a hot grill for 5–8 minutes, turning once. Set aside for 1–2 minutes, then serve with mango chutney, and chapattis, naans or boiled rice.

Quick Keema Matar

Heat 2 tablespoons vegetable oil in a large frying pan, then add 3 tablespoons madras curry paste and cook for 1 minute. Add 500 g (1 lb) minced lamb and cook for 2–3 minutes, until browned all over. Stir in 150 g (5 oz) frozen peas and 2 chopped tomatoes, season with salt and pepper, then pour in 250 ml (8 fl oz) boiling water. Bring to the boil, reduce the heat and simmer gently for about 15 minutes, until cooked and thickened. Serve hot with mango chutney, and chapattis, naans or boiled rice.

Chorizo and Butter Bean Salad

Serves 4

2 tablespoons olive or
  vegetable oil
1 red onion, finely sliced
100 g (3½ oz) chorizo, sliced
1 teaspoon paprika
2 x 400 g (13 oz) cans butter
  beans, drained and rinsed
3 tablespoons roughly chopped
  parsley
2 tablespoons sherry or red
  wine vinegar
3 ripe tomatoes, chopped
salt and pepper

- Heat the oil in a large frying pan and cook the onion over a medium-high heat for 2–3 minutes, until starting to colour. Add the chorizo and cook for 1–2 minutes, until golden. Stir in the paprika and butter beans, and cook for a further 1–2 minutes.

- Add the parsley, vinegar and chopped tomatoes to the pan, toss well, then remove from the heat. Season to taste and spoon into 4 shallow bowls to serve.

20 Warm Chorizo and Broad Bean Salad
Cook 500 g (1 lb) frozen broad beans in a large saucepan of lightly salted boiling water for 3–4 minutes, until tender. Drain, refresh under cold running water, then remove the skins from the beans. Follow the main recipe, replacing the butter beans with the broad beans.

30 Chorizo and Broad Bean Bake Follow the 20-minute recipe, then tip the beans and sauce into an ovenproof dish. Mix 100 g (3½ oz) fresh breadcrumbs with 3 tablespoons grated Parmesan-style cheese and 3 tablespoons roughly chopped parsley. Scatter over the beans, drizzle with 1 tablespoon oil and cook under a preheated grill for 7–8 minutes, until crisp and golden. Serve with green salad.

BUD-MEAT-SIC

Pork, Mushroom and Lemon Tagliatelle

Serves 4

400 g (13 oz) tagliatelle pasta
2 tablespoons olive or
   vegetable oil
300 g (10 oz) pork fillet, cut into
   thin strips
300 g (10 oz) field mushrooms,
   sliced
100 ml (3½ fl oz) dry white wine
1 teaspoon dried tarragon
200 ml (7 fl oz) double cream
salt and pepper
1 lemon, sliced, to garnish

- Cook the tagliatelle in a large saucepan of lightly salted boiling water for 8 minutes, or according to packet instructions, until al dente.

- Meanwhile, heat the oil in a deep-sided frying pan and fry the pork strips for 6–7 minutes, until golden. Remove with a slotted spoon and set aside in a bowl.

- Add the mushrooms to the pan and cook for 3–4 minutes, until soft and golden. Remove and add to the pork.

- If using the lemon, arrange the slices in a single layer in the pan and cook for 2–3 minutes, turning once, until golden. Remove and set aside.

- Pour the wine and tarragon into the pan, and bubble to reduce by half. Return the mushroom and pork to the pan and pour in the cream. Season well. Simmer gently for 2–3 minutes, until thickened slightly, then serve immediately alongside the tagliatelle, garnished with the lemon slices.

---

10 Bacon and Mushroom Tagliatelle Cook 400 g (13 oz) quick-cook tagliatelle according to packet instructions. Heat 2 tablespoons oil in a frying pan and cook 200 g (7 oz) chopped thick-cut bacon for 3–4 minutes. Add 300 g (10 oz) sliced field mushrooms and cook for 3–4 minutes. Stir in 2 teaspoons chopped fresh tarragon and 275 ml (9 fl oz) single cream, then season and bring to the boil. Stir in 1 tablespoon lemon juice and serve with the tagliatelle.

30 Creamy Pork and Mushroom Stroganoff Cook 400 g (13 oz) tagliatelle according to the packet instructions. Heat 2 tablespoons olive or vegetable oil in a large frying pan and cook 350 g (11½ oz) pork strips for 4–5 minutes, until cooked and golden. Remove with a slotted spoon and set aside. Return the pan to the heat, and add 1 sliced onion and 2 chopped garlic cloves and cook gently for 7–8 minutes, until softened and lightly golden. Add 300 g (10 oz) sliced field mushrooms and fry gently for a further 5–6 minutes. Stir in 2 teaspoons paprika, cook for 1 minute, then add 275 ml (9 fl oz) soured cream and bring to a gentle simmer. Season to taste, then return the pork and any juices to the pan for 1–2 minutes, until hot. Stir in 2 teaspoons lemon juice and 2 tablespoons chopped parsley, and serve immediately with tagliatelle.

Marinated Beef Chow Mein with Broccoli

Serves 4

300 g (10 oz) stir-fry beef strips, or rump steak, cut into strips
1 tablespoon dark soy sauce
3 tablespoons Chinese rice wine or dry sherry
1 teaspoon Chinese five-spice powder
2 tablespoons cornflour
½ teaspoon sugar
200 g (7 oz) medium dried egg noodles
3 tablespoons vegetable oil
1 onion, halved and thinly sliced
1 red pepper, cored, deseeded and thinly sliced
250 g (8 oz) small broccoli florets
2 garlic cloves, thinly sliced
2.5-cm (1-inch) piece of fresh root ginger, cut into matchsticks
4 tablespoons oyster sauce
100 ml (3½ fl oz) water

- Mix the beef with the soy sauce, rice wine, five-spice powder, cornflour and sugar, and set aside to marinate for 15–20 minutes.

- Bring a large saucepan of water to the boil, add the egg noodles and immediately remove from the heat. Cover and set aside for 4–5 minutes, until tender. Alternatively, cook according to packet instructions. Drain and cool under running water. Drain well, then toss with 1 tablespoon of the oil.

- Heat the remaining oil in a large wok or frying pan, and stir-fry the onion and pepper for 2–3 minutes, until softened slightly, then stir in the broccoli florets and cook for a further 2–3 minutes. Add the garlic and ginger, and cook for 1 minute, stirring frequently.

- Tip the beef and its marinade into the pan and stir-fry for 3–4 minutes, until well browned. Pour in the oyster sauce and measured water, then add the noodles. Simmer gently for 2–3 minutes, until the noodles are hot. Heap into shallow bowls and serve immediately.

 Beef and Vegetable Chow Mein Heat 3 tablespoons vegetable oil in a wok, add 300 g (10 oz) stir-fry beef strips and cook for 1–2 minutes, until just browned. Add 600 g (1 lb 3½ oz) ready-prepared stir-fry vegetables and cook for 3–4 minutes, until beginning to soften. Stir in 400 g (13 oz) straight-to-wok egg noodles and 350 g (11½ oz) chow mein stir-fry sauce, and cook for 2–3 minutes. Serve in bowls.

Beef and Black Bean Chow Mein with Pak Choi Cook 200 g (7 oz) medium dried egg noodles following the main recipe. Heat 2 tablespoons vegetable oil in a large wok or frying pan and add 300 g (10 oz) rump steak, cut into strips. Cook for 2–3 minutes, stirring frequently, until sealed and almost cooked. Remove with a slotted spoon and set aside. Add 3 sliced spring onions and 1 sliced yellow pepper to the pan, and cook for 2–3 minutes, then stir in 250 g (8 oz) thickly sliced pak choi and cook for a further 2–3 minutes. Add the garlic and ginger, and cook for 1 minute, stirring frequently, then add 350 g (11½ oz) black bean stir-fry sauce and simmer for 2 minutes before returning the beef and noodles to the pan. Cook for 1–2 minutes, until hot, then heap into bowls to serve.

Grilled Macaroni Cheese with Bacon

Serves 4

300 g (10 oz) macaroni pasta

2 tablespoons olive or vegetable oil

150 g (5 oz) smoked streaky bacon, chopped

100 g (3½ oz) mushrooms, sliced or chopped

500 ml (17 fl oz) milk

50 g (2 oz) plain flour

50 g (2 oz) butter

150 g (5 oz) medium or mature Cheddar cheese, grated

pinch of ground nutmeg (optional)

freshly ground black pepper

- Cook the macaroni in a large saucepan of lightly salted boiling water for 8–10 minutes, or according to packet instructions, until al dente.

- Meanwhile, heat the oil in a frying pan and cook the bacon for 3–4 minutes, until cooked and lightly golden. Add the mushrooms and cook for a further 3–4 minutes, until softened. Remove from the heat and set aside.

- Pour the milk into a saucepan with the flour and butter, and cook over a medium heat, whisking constantly, until thickened and simmering gently. Cook for 2–3 minutes, then remove from the heat and stir in half the grated cheese.

- Drain the pasta and combine with the cheese sauce, bacon and mushrooms. Add the nutmeg, if using, and season with black pepper. Tip into a large ovenproof dish, scatter over the remaining cheese and cook under a preheated grill for 5–6 minutes, until golden and bubbling. Serve immediately.

Cheesy Mushroom and Ham Macaroni

Cook 400 g (13 oz) quick-cook macaroni according to packet instructions. Meanwhile, heat 2 tablespoons oil in a deep-sided frying pan and cook 100 g (3½ oz) sliced mushrooms for 3–4 minutes, until softened. Add 275 ml (9 fl oz) double cream, 150 g (5 oz) chopped ham, 150 g (5 oz) grated medium or mature Cheddar cheese, a pinch of ground nutmeg and seasoning, and heat until bubbling gently. Drain the pasta, stir into the sauce and serve immediately.

Baked Cheese and Ham Macaroni

Cook 800 g (1 lb 10 oz) fresh spinach and ricotta-filled pasta in a large saucepan of lightly salted boiling water for 2–3 minutes, or according to packet instructions, until not quite tender. Meanwhile, make the cheese sauce following the main recipe. Stir 150 g (5 oz) chopped ham and a 285 g (9½ oz) can drained, sliced mushrooms into the cheese sauce, then stir into the pasta. Tip into a large ovenproof dish, then sprinkle over the remaining cheese and bake in a preheated oven, 190°C (375°F), Gas Mark 5, for about 20 minutes, until bubbling and golden. Serve with crunchy green salad.

 # Fried Steak with Green Peppercorn Sauce

Serves 4

2 tablespoons olive oil

4 feather steaks, approximately 125 g (4 oz) each

25 g (1 oz) butter

125 ml (4 fl oz) single cream

2 teaspoons green peppercorns in water, drained

salt and pepper

To serve

green salad

crusty bread or chips

- Heat the oil in a large nonstick frying pan and fry the steaks for 1–3 minutes on each side, depending on how you like your steak. Season to taste with salt and pepper, remove the steaks from the pan and transfer to a warm ovenproof dish to rest.

- Add the butter, cream and peppercorns to the pan, and bubble over a medium-low heat for 1–2 minutes, scraping the pan to loosen any tasty bits.

- Serve the steaks drizzled with the sauce, accompanied by green salad and bread or chips.

 Green Peppercorn Burgers with Blue Cheese Sauce Place 400 g (13 oz) minced beef in a bowl with 1 chopped red onion, 2 teaspoons green peppercorns in water, drained, 25 g (1 oz) ready-made natural dried breadcrumbs, 1 beaten egg and 1 tablespoon finely chopped parsley or chives, then season and mix to combine. Form into 4 burgers, then heat 2 tablespoons olive oil in a frying pan and cook for 4–5 minutes on each side, until cooked through. Meanwhile, place 100 g (3½ oz) creamy blue cheese in a small bowl with 2 tablespoons crème fraîche and lots of black pepper. Mash together until smooth and serve on buns with the burgers and some slices of fresh tomato.

Beef and Green Peppercorn Goulash Heat 2 tablespoons olive oil in a large nonstick frying pan and add 350 g (11½ oz) sliced beef. Cook over a medium-high heat for 3–4 minutes, until browned all over, then remove with a slotted spoon and set aside. Reduce the heat slightly and add 1 extra tablespoon of oil, then cook 1 sliced onion, 1 sliced red or green pepper and 2 chopped garlic cloves for 6–7 minutes, until softened and lightly coloured. Stir in 1 tablespoon plain flour and 1 tablespoon paprika, cook for 1 minute, then pour in a 400 g (13 oz) can chopped tomatoes, 1 tablespoon tomato purée, 300 ml (½ pint) hot beef or vegetable stock, 2 teaspoons green peppercorns in water, drained, and seasoning to taste. Bring to the boil and simmer gently for 15–18 minutes, until rich and thick. Return the beef to the pan with any juices and stir to heat through. Stir in 125 ml (4 fl oz) single cream and serve with boiled rice and chopped parsley, to garnish.

30 Baked Chicken with Lime

Serves 4

2 limes

2.5-cm (1-inch) piece of fresh root
   ginger, peeled and finely grated

1 teaspoon Thai fish sauce

1 tablespoon groundnut or
   vegetable oil

1 large bunch of coriander

4 chicken breasts, about 150 g
   (5 oz) each

350 g (11½ oz) Thai rice, rinsed

600 ml (1 pint) cold water

salt

- Preheat the oven to 200°C (400°F), Gas Mark 6, and line a roasting tin with foil. Finely grate the rind from the 2 limes, squeeze the juice from one of them and finely slice the other.

- Place the lime rind and juice in a mini-chopper or the small bowl of a food processor with the ginger, fish sauce, oil and the coriander, including the stalks. Blend to make a paste.

- Cut 3 deep slashes diagonally into the chicken breasts and massage the paste all over the chicken. Place a slice of lime into each slash.

- Place the chicken breasts in the roasting tin, cover with foil and bake in the preheated oven for 18–20 minutes, until the chicken is cooked through.

- Meanwhile, place the rice in a large saucepan with the measured water, season with salt and bring to the boil. Reduce the heat, cover with a tight-fitting lid and cook very gently for 15–18 minutes, until all of the water has been absorbed and the rice is tender and sticky. Serve the chicken with the sticky rice, drizzled with chicken juices.

 Chicken and Lime Noodle Salad Place 375 g (12 oz) cooked and cooled rice noodles in a bowl with 300 g (10 oz) cooked chicken strips, grated rind of 1 lime, 1 bunch of coriander, chopped, and 1 thinly sliced red pepper, and toss to combine. Pour 3 tablespoons vegetable oil into a small bowl with 2 tablespoons lime juice, 2 teaspoons grated ginger and 1 tablespoon fish sauce, and whisk to combine. Drizzle the salad with the dressing to serve.

Chicken and Lime Stir-Fry Cook 350 g (11½ oz) Thai rice following the main recipe. Heat 1 tablespoon groundnut or vegetable oil in a large nonstick frying pan and add 400 g (13 oz) sliced chicken thigh meat. Stir-fry for 7–8 minutes, until cooked and golden, then add 1 sliced red pepper, 1 tablespoon chopped ginger and 3 thickly sliced spring onions. Stir-fry for a further 3–4 minutes, until softened. Meanwhile, mix together 2 tablespoons honey, 2 tablespoons light soy sauce, 1 teaspoon sesame oil and 2 tablespoons lime juice. Stir this sauce into the pan, cook for 30 seconds, then spoon over the cooked rice to serve.

BUD-MEAT-CUY

Warm Tomato, Liver and Bacon Salad

Serves 4

2 tablespoons olive oil

150 g (5 oz) smoked streaky bacon, chopped

250 g (8 oz) chicken livers, trimmed

4 ripe tomatoes, sliced

125 g (4 oz) watercress or lambs' lettuce

½ red onion, halved and sliced

salt and pepper

For the dressing

3 tablespoons olive oil

1 tablespoon red wine vinegar

1 teaspoon Dijon mustard

pinch of sugar

- Heat the oil in a nonstick frying pan and cook the bacon for 3–4 minutes, until crisp and golden. Remove from the pan with a slotted spoon and set aside. Season the chicken livers with salt and pepper, and add to the hot pan. Cook for 4–5 minutes, until browned and cooked through.

- Combine all the dressing ingredients in a jar with a tight-fitting lid and shake well.

- Arrange the tomatoes on 4 plates with the watercress and red onion. Scatter the liver and bacon over the prepared salads and serve immediately, drizzled with the dressing.

2 Liver and Bacon Tagliatelle

Cook 500 g (1 lb) tagliatelle according to packet instructions. Heat 2 tablespoons oil in a frying pan and cook 150 g (5 oz) chopped smoked streaky bacon for 3–4 minutes. Add 1 chopped red onion and 2 chopped garlic cloves. Cook for 4–5 minutes. Add 250 g (8 oz) chicken livers, trimmed, and fry for 2–3 minutes to brown, then add 2 tablespoons dry sherry, scraping the bottom of the pan to loosen any bits. Add 200 ml (7 fl oz) single cream, 4 chopped sun-dried tomatoes and 1 teaspoon dried sage. Season and simmer for 2–3 minutes, until the livers are just cooked. Serve with the tagliatelle.

3 Crispy Potatoes with Liver and Bacon

Cook 450 g (14½ oz) waxy new potatoes in a saucepan of lightly salted boiling water for about 10 minutes, until almost tender. Drain well, toss with 2 tablespoons oil, then tip into a roasting tin and cook in a preheated oven, 220°C (425°F), Gas Mark 7, for 15–20 minutes, shaking occasionally, until crisp and golden. Meanwhile, cook 150 g (5 oz) chopped smoked streaky bacon, 1 chopped red onion, 2 chopped garlic cloves and 250 g (8 oz) chicken livers, following the 20-minute recipe. Once the chicken livers have browned, sprinkle 1 tablespoon plain flour into the pan with 1 tablespoon tomato purée, cook for 1 minute then add 2 tablespoons Madeira, if desired, followed by 150 ml (¼ pint) hot chicken stock. Simmer gently for 3–4 minutes, until the sauce has thickened slightly and the livers are just cooked through. Remove from the heat, stir the cooked potatoes and 2 teaspoons chopped sage leaves into the pan, then season to taste and spoon into 4 shallow dishes. Serve immediately with the watercress and tomatoes.

 Beef Pies with Crunchy Topping

Serves 4

500 g (1 lb) floury potatoes, peeled and cut into chunks
2 tablespoons olive oil
450 g (14½ oz) frying steak, sliced
2 garlic cloves, chopped
1 leek, sliced
350 g (11½ oz) mushrooms, quartered
75 g (3 oz) butter
2 teaspoons paprika
1 tablespoon tomato purée
140 ml (4½ fl oz) double cream
1 beef stock cube
150 ml (¼ pint) water
50 g (2 oz) fresh breadcrumbs
2 tablespoons chopped chives
125 g (4 oz) Cheddar cheese, grated
salt and pepper

- Cook the potatoes in a large saucepan of lightly salted boiling water for 12–15 minutes, until tender.

- Meanwhile, heat the oil in a large pan and cook the steak for 3–4 minutes, until browned all over, then remove from the pan and set aside. Add the garlic, leek and mushrooms to the pan with one-third of the butter, and cook for 7–8 minutes. Stir in the paprika and tomato purée, followed by the cream, stock cube and measured water. Bring to the boil and simmer gently for 5–6 minutes to thicken slightly.

- Drain the potatoes and return to the pan over a low heat to remove excess moisture. Turn off the heat, then mash the potatoes until smooth with the remaining butter. Season. Mix the breadcrumbs with the chives and Cheddar. Stir the beef and any juices back into the mushrooms, then divide between 4 individual pie dishes. Top each pie with mashed potatoes, then the topping. Cook the pies under a preheated grill for 5–6 minutes, until bubbling, golden and crunchy. Serve hot.

1 Steaks with Crunchy-Topped

Mash Mix 50 g (2 oz) fresh breadcrumbs with 2 tablespoons chopped chives and 125 g (4 oz) grated Cheddar. Place 850 g (1 lb 11½ oz) ready-made mashed potato in a small ovenproof dish and scatter over the topping. Cook under a preheated grill for 5–6 minutes. Meanwhile, heat a griddle pan. Rub 1 tablespoon oil over 4 frying steaks, about 125 g (4 oz) each, and cook for 1–3 minutes on each side. Serve with the crunchy-topped mash and steamed broccoli.

2 Cheat's Crunchy-Topped Cottage

Pie Heat 1 tablespoon olive oil and 25 g (1 oz) butter in a large saucepan, and cook 200 g (7 oz) mushrooms with 2 chopped garlic cloves and 1 sliced leek for 7–8 minutes, until softened and lightly golden. Mix 50 g (2 oz) fresh breadcrumbs in a bowl with 2 tablespoons chopped chives and 125 g (4 oz) coarsely grated Cheddar cheese. Stir in a 400 g (13 oz) can baked beans in tomato sauce and 400 g (13 oz) crumbled corned beef into the mushroom mixture, and heat through thoroughly. Tip into an ovenproof dish and top with 500 g (1 lb) warmed ready-made carrot and swede or potato mash. Sprinkle over the breadcrumb topping and cook under the grill for 5–6 minutes, until golden and crunchy. Serve with steamed broccoli.

Herby Sausages with Potato and Celeriac Mash

Serves 4

600 g (1 lb 3½ oz) floury potatoes, peeled and diced

400 g (13 oz) celeriac, peeled and diced

8 country-style pork and herb sausages

50 g (2 oz) butter

1 tablespoon chopped thyme leaves

salt and pepper

steamed carrots, to serve

- Cook the potato and celeriac in a large saucepan of lightly salted boiling water for about 15 minutes, until tender. Drain, then return to the pan and place over a low heat for 30 seconds to remove excess liquid.

- Meanwhile, cook the sausages under a preheated grill for 12–15 minutes, turning occasionally, until cooked and golden.

- Mash the potato and celeriac with the butter, thyme and plenty of seasoning. Serve the grilled sausages with the mash and some steamed carrots.

Herby Sausages with Celeriac Remoulade

Heat 1 tablespoon olive or vegetable oil in a frying pan and cook 12 pork and herb chipolatas for about 8 minutes, turning occasionally, until cooked through and golden. Meanwhile, coarsely grate 575 g (1 lb 3 oz) peeled celeriac and toss with 1 tablespoon lemon juice. Add 5 tablespoons mayonnaise, 2 tablespoons wholegrain mustard and a pinch of sugar, season to taste and mix well to combine. Spoon on to plates and serve with the cooked sausages.

Potato and Celeriac Soup with Sausage Croûtons

Melt the butter in a large saucepan with 1 tablespoon oil, and add 1 chopped onion and 2 chopped garlic cloves. Cook for 6–7 minutes, until softened and lightly coloured. Add 400 g (13 oz) diced celeriac and 400 g (13 oz) diced potato, and cook for 3–4 minutes, until lightly golden. Stir in 1.2 litres (2 pints) hot vegetable stock and most of 1 tablespoon chopped thyme leaves, reserving 1 teaspoon to garnish. Season and bring to the boil, then reduce the heat and simmer gently for about 15 minutes, until the celeriac and potato are really tender. Meanwhile, heat 1 tablespoon oil in a frying pan and cook 4 chopped pork and herb sausages for 8–10 minutes, until really crisp and golden. Drain on kitchen paper and set aside. Blend the soup using a hand-held blender and ladle into bowls. Scatter over the crispy sausage pieces and the remaining thyme to serve.

Creamy Cider Chicken with Rice

Serves 4

3 tablespoons olive or vegetable oil

8 boneless chicken thighs, about 625 g (1¼ lb) total weight

2–3 tablespoons seasoned flour

100 g (3½ oz) back bacon, chopped

100 g (3½ oz) mushrooms, sliced

200 ml (7 fl oz) boiling vegetable or chicken stock

250 ml (8 fl oz) dry cider

2 tablespoons cider vinegar

400 g (13 oz) long-grain rice

4 tablespoons single cream or crème fraîche

salt and pepper

- Heat 2 tablespoons of the oil in a large, deep-sided frying pan. Dust the chicken with the seasoned flour and cook in the pan, skin side down, for about 10 minutes, until really golden and crisp.

- Meanwhile, heat the remaining oil in a small frying pan and cook the bacon for 3–4 minutes, until golden. Add the mushrooms and cook for a further 2–3 minutes, until softened.

- Turn the chicken thighs over, then add the bacon and mushrooms to the pan. Pour over the stock, cider and cider vinegar, bring to the boil, then reduce the heat and simmer gently for about 15 minutes, until the chicken is cooked.

- Meanwhile, cook the rice according to packet instructions, then drain and divide between 4 shallow dishes.

- Arrange the chicken thighs alongside the rice, then stir the cream into the pan. Season to taste with salt and pepper, then spoon the sauce over the chicken to serve.

10 Creamy Chicken Rice

Heat 2 tablespoons oil in a frying pan and cook 100 g (3½ oz) chopped back bacon for 3–4 minutes, until golden. Add 100 g (3½ oz) sliced mushrooms and cook for 2–3 minutes more. Add 300 g (10 oz) diced, cooked chicken, 500 g (1 lb) cooked rice and 300 ml (½ pint) crème fraîche, then season well and stir over the heat for 1–2 minutes, until hot. Spoon the creamy rice into 4 bowls to serve.

20 Quick Creamy Cider Chicken

For a quicker version of the main recipe, remove the skin and slice 8 boneless chicken thighs. Heat 2 tablespoons oil in a large pan and cook the chicken for 5–6 minutes, until golden. Meanwhile, cook 400 g (13 oz) long-grain rice in a large saucepan of lightly salted boiling water for about 12 minutes, or according to packet instructions. Add 100 g (3½ oz) chopped back bacon to the chicken and cook for 3–4 minutes, then stir in 100 g (3½ oz) sliced mushrooms and cook for a further 2–3 minutes. Pour in 250 ml (8 fl oz) dry cider and 1 tablespoon cider vinegar, and simmer gently for 7–8 minutes, until the chicken is cooked and the cider has reduced slightly. Remove from the heat, pour in 4 tablespoons single cream or crème fraîche, season to taste and serve spooned over the cooked rice.

 # Deconstructed Shepherd's Pie

Serves 4

1 onion, roughly chopped

1 large carrot, roughly chopped

1 celery stick, roughly chopped

2 garlic cloves

2 tablespoons vegetable oil

400 g (13 oz) minced lamb

2 tablespoons plain flour

250 ml (8 fl oz) hot lamb or vegetable stock

400 g (13 oz) can chopped tomatoes

1 tablespoon tomato ketchup

1 tablespoon Worcestershire sauce

2–3 bay leaves (optional)

1 kg (2 lb) floury potatoes, peeled and roughly diced

50 g (2 oz) butter

3–4 tablespoons milk

salt and pepper

- Place the onion, carrot, celery and garlic in a food processor and pulse quickly until finely chopped. Heat the oil in a large, deep-sided frying pan or casserole and cook the chopped vegetables for about 8 minutes, until tender and lightly golden. Add the meat and cook over a high heat, stirring occasionally, for 2–3 minutes, until browned all over.

- Sprinkle over the flour and stir well. Pour in the stock, then add the chopped tomatoes, tomato ketchup, Worcestershire sauce, bay leaves, if using, and plenty of seasoning. Bring to the boil, then reduce the heat slightly, cover and simmer for 15–18 minutes, until thickened.

- Meanwhile, cook the potatoes in a large saucepan of lightly salted boiling water for about 15 minutes, until tender. Drain the potatoes, return them to the pan with the butter and mash until smooth over a very low heat. Stir in the milk and season to taste.

- Remove and discard the bay leaves, spoon the meat sauce into bowls and serve immediately with the mashed potatoes.

---

1 Shepherd's Lamb with Couscous

Rub 1 tablespoon olive oil over 4 lamb steaks, about 125 g (4 oz) each. Sprinkle over 1 teaspoon dried rosemary and a pinch of salt and pepper. Heat a nonstick frying pan and cook the lamb steaks for 2–4 minutes each side, depending on how you like your lamb. Meanwhile, pour 300 ml (½ pint) boiling water over 250 g (8 oz) Mediterranean-flavoured couscous, then cover and set aside for 5–8 minutes, or according to the packet instructions, until the liquid has been absorbed and the grains are tender. Spoon the couscous on to 4 warmed plates and serve with the lamb steaks and lemon wedges.

2 Fast Shepherd's Pie Heat

2 tablespoons vegetable oil in a frying pan and fry 400 g (13 oz) minced lamb for 7–8 minutes, until browned, then add 500 g (1 lb) ready-made chunky vegetable pasta sauce. Simmer for 3–4 minutes, then pour into an ovenproof dish and top with 750 g (1½ lb) ready-made, warmed mashed potato. Sprinkle with 125 g (4 oz) grated Cheddar and cook under a preheated grill for 6–7 minutes, until golden.

Cajun-Spiced Hot Dogs

Serves 4

2 tablespoons vegetable oil

1 red onion, halved and sliced

2 red peppers, or 1 red and 1 yellow, cored, deseeded and sliced

8 chicken or pork frankfurter sausages

1 tablespoon Cajun seasoning mix

To serve

8 long bread rolls, warmed

ready-made salsa (optional)

- Heat the oil in a large nonstick frying pan, and cook the onions and peppers over a high heat for 6–7 minutes, until slightly charred.

- Reduce the heat slightly and add the frankfurters and Cajun spices. Cook for 2–3 minutes, until hot. Serve the sausages and cooked vegetables in warmed rolls with salsa, if desired.

Cajun-Spiced Sausage Fajitas

Cook 8 pork sausages under a preheated grill for 12 minutes, turning frequently, until cooked through and golden. Meanwhile, heat 2 tablespoons vegetable oil in a frying pan, and cook 1 halved and sliced red onion and 2 sliced red peppers over a high heat for 6–7 minutes, until slightly charred. Thickly slice the sausages diagonally and add to the pan with 1 tablespoon Cajun seasoning mix, stirring frequently for 2–3 minutes, until the sausages are golden. Divide the mixture between 4–8 soft flour tortillas. Top with 150 g (5 oz) grated Cheddar cheese, 1 small, shredded iceberg lettuce and some ready-made salsa. Roll up the tortillas, cut in half and serve immediately.

Cajun-Roasted Sausages with Rice and Tortillas

Cut 8 tomato and chilli or plain pork sausages into 3.5-cm (1½-inch) pieces and place in a bowl with 2 diced red peppers, 1 diced aubergine and 1 red onion, cut into thin wedges. Add 3 tablespoons oil and 2 tablespoons Cajun seasoning mix, toss well together, then tip on to a large baking sheet. Cook in a preheated oven, 230°C (450°F), Gas Mark 8, for 20–25 minutes, turning occasionally, until the sausages are cooked and the vegetables slightly softened. Meanwhile, cook 350 g (11½ oz) long-grain rice in a large saucepan of lightly salted boiling water for about 12 minutes, or according to packet instructions, until just tender. Serve the Cajun-roasted sausages with the cooked rice, soft flour tortillas and salsa.

BUD-MEAT-JEQ

Double Whammy Beef Burgers with Pickles

Serves 4

450 g (14½ oz) minced beef
1 onion, finely chopped
50 g (2 oz) fresh breadcrumbs
½ teaspoon dried garlic powder
1 egg, lightly beaten
2 tablespoons olive or
   vegetable oil
4 large bread rolls
4 thin slices of Cheddar cheese
3–4 large American-style pickles
   (gherkins), sliced
salt and pepper

To serve

125 g (4 oz) mixed salad leaves
barbecue sauce (optional)

- Place the minced beef in a bowl with the onion, breadcrumbs, garlic powder and egg. Season to taste with salt and pepper, mix to combine, then form into 8 thin burgers.

- Heat the oil in a large nonstick frying pan and cook the burgers for 3–4 minutes on each side, until cooked and golden.

- Arrange mixed salad leaves on the bottom half of each bread roll and top with sliced pickles, a burger, a slice of cheese, a second burger, barbecue sauce, if desired, and another layer of pickles, before replacing the lids.

American-Style Open Beef Sandwiches Halve a French stick horizontally and cut each piece in half to create 4 lengths. Toast under a preheated grill, cut side up, for about 2 minutes, until just golden. Mix 1 tablespoon creamed horseradish with 3 tablespoons mayonnaise and spread on the pieces of bread. Scatter over 125 g (4 oz) mixed salad leaves, then top with 3–4 sliced large American-style pickles. Arrange 150 g (5 oz) thinly sliced roast beef or corned beef on top, scatter with ½ a thinly sliced red onion and serve immediately.

Cheesy Corned Beef Hash Parboil 500 g (1 lb) potatoes, cut into bite-sized chunks, in a large saucepan of lightly salted boiling water for 7–8 minutes, then drain. Meanwhile, heat 2 tablespoons olive or vegetable oil in a large nonstick frying pan, and cook 1 finely chopped onion and 2 chopped garlic cloves for 8–9 minutes, until soft and golden. Crumble 340 g (11¼ oz) corned beef into the bottom of a lightly greased ovenproof dish and top with the cooked onions. Clean the pan, then return to the heat with 2 extra tablespoons oil and fry the potatoes gently for 7–8 minutes, turning frequently, until golden and tender. Arrange 3–4 sliced large American-style pickles and 8 thin slices of Cheddar cheese over the onions and scatter with the potatoes. Cook in a preheated oven, 230°C (450°F), Gas Mark 8, for 10–12 minutes until hot and crispy. Meanwhile, poach 4 eggs in a large pan of simmering water for 3 minutes. Serve the corned beef hash with the poached eggs and mixed salad leaves.

Golden Pork Chops with Parsnip and Apple Mash

Serves 4

1 kg (2 lb) parsnips, peeled and
  cut into chunks
325 g (11 oz) cooking apples,
  peeled, cored and cut into
  chunks
1 tablespoon olive or vegetable oil
4 thick-cut pork chops, about
  200 g (7 oz) each
100 g (3½ oz) butter
100 ml (3½ fl oz) whole milk
  or single cream
1 tablespoon chopped sage
pinch of ground nutmeg
100 g (3½ oz) taleggio or
  mozzarella cheese, cut into
  8 slices
salt and pepper
steamed green beans, to serve

- Cook the parsnips in a large saucepan of lightly salted boiling water for about 15 minutes, adding the apples after 5 minutes, until both are tender.

- Rub the oil over the pork chops, season well, then cook on a foil-lined grill rack under a preheated grill for 15–18 minutes, turning once, until cooked through and golden.

- Drain the parsnips and apples, then return to the pan and place over a low heat for 1–2 minutes to remove excess moisture. Remove from the heat and mash really well with the butter and milk. Add the sage and nutmeg, season to taste and beat until smooth. Keep warm.

- Top each pork chop with 2 slices of cheese, return to the grill and cook for 2–3 minutes, until melted and golden.

- Spoon the mash on to 4 warmed plates, and serve with the golden pork chops and steamed green beans.

Golden Bacon, Apple and Taleggio

Toasties Cook 8 slices of back bacon under a preheated grill for 5–6 minutes, until crisp and golden. Meanwhile, lightly toast 4 thick slices of bread in a toaster. Spread each slice with 1 tablespoon apple sauce, then top with the bacon, followed by 100 g (3½ oz) sliced taleggio cheese. Return to the grill for 2–3 minutes, until melting and golden. Serve immediately with green salad.

Golden Pork with Caramelized

Apples and Parsnip Mash Cook 500 g (1 lb) potatoes and 500 g (1 lb) parsnips, peeled and cut into chunks, in a large saucepan of lightly salted boiling water for 12–15 minutes, until tender. Drain, return to the pan and mash with 50 g (2 oz) butter and 1 tablespoon chopped sage and a pinch of ground nutmeg. Meanwhile, core 2 eating apples and cut each into 8 wedges. Heat 50 g (2 oz) butter in a large nonstick frying pan, add the apple wedges and cook for 8–10 minutes, until soft and slightly caramelized. Wipe the pan and return to the heat. Add 1 tablespoon olive or vegetable oil and cook 4 thin-cut pork loin steaks, about 125 g (4 oz) each, for 4–5 minutes each side, until golden and cooked through. Spoon the mash on to 4 plates, arrange the pork steaks by the side and top with the caramelized apples to serve.

Turkey Milanese with Aioli and Garlic Bread

Serves 4

4 turkey breast escalopes, about 125 g (4 oz) each
2 small eggs, beaten
3 tablespoons seasoned flour
100 g (3½ oz) fresh breadcrumbs
2 small garlic cloves, crushed
50 g (2 oz) butter, softened
2 tablespoons finely chopped parsley
1 small French stick or ciabatta loaf
3 tablespoons vegetable oil
salt and pepper
lemon wedge, to garnish
salad leaves, to serve

For the aioli

1 large egg yolk
½ teaspoon crushed garlic
1 teaspoon white wine vinegar
½ teaspoon Dijon mustard
150 ml (¼ pint) vegetable oil

- Place the turkey escalopes, one at a time, between 2 pieces of clingfilm and beat with a rolling pin until about 1 cm (½ inch) thick. Put the beaten eggs in a large, shallow bowl, and place the seasoned flour and breadcrumbs on 2 separate plates. Coat the turkey on both sides in the seasoned flour, followed by the egg and finally the breadcrumbs. Set aside. Preheat the oven to 200°C (400°F), Gas Mark 6.

- To make the aioli, place the egg yolk in a mini-chopper or the small bowl of a food processor with the ½ teaspoon crushed garlic, vinegar and mustard, and pulse to combine. Add the oil in a slow, steady stream, blending constantly until the mixture has the consistency of mayonnaise. Season to taste.

- Mash the 2 garlic cloves into the butter with the parsley. Cut slices into the bread loaf, not quite cutting all the way through, then spread the garlic butter on to all the cut sides. Wrap in foil and place in the preheated oven for 5 minutes, then open the foil and cook for a further 2–3 minutes.

- Meanwhile, heat the oil in a large nonstick frying pan and cook the escalopes for 3–4 minutes on each side, until cooked through. Serve with salad leaves, the garlic bread and aioli and garnish with a lemon wedge.

1 **Garlicky Turkey Bagels** Split and toast 4 bagels and spread the cut sides with 2–4 tablespoons ready-made garlic mayonnaise. Place the bottom halves on 4 plates and divide 200 (7 oz) wafer-thin smoked turkey between them. Top each with a slice of Cheddar cheese and a handful of salad leaves, then add a little thinly sliced red onion. Replace the tops and serve cut in half.

2 **Turkey Saltimbocca with Garlic Bread** Beat 4 turkey escalopes to flatten them, following the main recipe. Mash 2 crushed garlic cloves into 50 g (2 oz) softened butter with 2 tablespoons chopped parsley. Spread the butter over the escalopes, then top each with 1 thin slice of Parma-style ham and secure with cocktail sticks. Dust each escalope with seasoned flour. Heat 3 tablespoons oil in a nonstick frying pan and cook the turkey for 2–3 minutes each side, until cooked through. Remove from the pan and place somewhere warm to rest for 1–2 minutes. Meanwhile, pour 125 ml (4 fl oz) dry white wine into the pan, scraping the base to deglaze, and simmer for 1–2 minutes to reduce. Arrange the turkey on 4 warmed plates and drizzle over the juices. Serve with green salad and ready-made garlic bread.

Minced Pork Balls with Sweet and Sour Sauce

Serves 4

500 g (1 lb) minced pork
2 spring onions, finely chopped, plus extra to garnish
1 teaspoon crushed garlic
2 teaspoons very finely chopped fresh root ginger
1 tablespoon cornflour
1 small egg white, whisked
3–4 tablespoons vegetable or groundnut oil
350 g (11½ oz) Thai rice
soy sauce, to serve (optional)

For the sweet and sour sauce

225 g (7½ oz) can pineapple chunks in juice
125 g (4 oz) tomato ketchup
2½ tablespoons light soft brown sugar
2 tablespoons malt vinegar
2 teaspoons light soy sauce

- Place the minced pork in a large bowl with the spring onions, garlic and ginger. Whisk the cornflour into the egg white and add to the pork, mixing until well combined. Form the mixture into 20–24 balls. Heat the oil in a large nonstick frying pan. Cook the meatballs for 10–12 minutes, turning occasionally, until cooked through and golden.

- Meanwhile, place the rice in a saucepan with 1½ times its volume of cold water. Bring to the boil, season, cover and simmer gently for 11–14 minutes, until the rice is tender and the liquid has been absorbed. Garnish with spring onions.

- To make the sweet and sour sauce, tip the pineapple and its juice into a mini-chopper or food processor and pulse until crushed but not smooth. Alternatively, chop finely by hand. Pour into a small pan with the remaining ingredients, then bring to the boil, reduce the heat and simmer gently for 5–7 minutes, until thickened.

- Drain the excess oil from the pan of meatballs, then pour the sauce into the pan and simmer for a minute or two until well coated. Spoon the meatballs and sauce over the rice and serve immediately with soy sauce, if desired.

 Sweet and Sour Pork Noodles

Heat 2 tablespoons oil in a nonstick frying pan and cook 350 g (11½ oz) pork strips for 6–7 minutes, until cooked and golden. Stir in 500 g (1 lb) chunky vegetable sweet and sour sauce and heat for 1–2 minutes, until bubbling. Toss the sweet and sour pork with 600 g (1 lb 3½ oz) hot straight-to-wok noodles, and heap into bowls to serve.

 Sweet and Sour Pork with Vegetables Cut 400 g (13 oz) lean pork into cubes. Place 350 g (11½ oz) Thai rice in a saucepan with 1½ times its volume of cold water, bring to the boil, season with salt, cover and simmer gently for 11–14 minutes, until the rice is tender and the liquid has been absorbed. Heat 2 tablespoons oil in a large nonstick frying pan and cook the pork for 2–3 minutes, until browned. Add 1 sliced onion and 1 sliced red pepper, and stir-fry for 3–4 minutes, until beginning to soften. Add 100 g (3½ oz) sliced mushrooms and cook for a further 3–4 minutes, until softened. Meanwhile, make the sweet and sour sauce following the main recipe, then add to the pork and simmer gently for 2–3 minutes, until the pork is cooked through. Serve with the cooked rice.

BUD-MEAT-FOV

Koftas with Chickpeas and Rice

Serves 4

2 tablespoons olive or
vegetable oil

1 onion, finely chopped

2 garlic cloves, finely chopped

1 teaspoon ground cumin

1 teaspoon ground coriander

½ teaspoon ground cinnamon

pinch of allspice (optional)

200 g (7 oz) long-grain rice

400 g (13 oz) can chickpeas,
drained and rinsed

400 g (13 oz) minced lamb

100 g (3½ oz) feta cheese,
crumbled

1 egg, beaten

1 bunch of coriander, chopped

salt and pepper

ready-made tzatziki, to serve

- Heat the oil in a small frying pan and cook the onion for 4–5 minutes. Add the garlic and cook for 3–4 minutes. Add the spices and cook for a further minute, then remove from the heat and season with black pepper.

- Cook the rice according to packet instructions, until tender.

- Meanwhile, place half the chickpeas in the bowl of a food processor and pulse to chop. Add the lamb and pulse to combine. Scrape into a large bowl and add the feta. Stir in the cooked onions, then add the egg and mix until just combined.

- Form the mixture into 16–20 balls, then thread on to 4 metal skewers and flatten each kofta gently. Place on a foil-lined grill rack and cook under a preheated grill for about 8 minutes, turning once, until cooked through and golden.

- Meanwhile, fold the remaining chickpeas and chopped coriander into the drained rice and spoon on to 4 plates. Serve with the rice and a spoonful of tzatziki.

Giant Koftas with Chickpea Salad

Chop 200 g (7 oz) chickpeas in a food processor with 2 spring onions, 1 teaspoon cumin, 1 teaspoon coriander and ½ teaspoon cinnamon. Add 400 g (13 oz) minced lamb and 1 egg. Season, then pulse. Form into 4 flattened sausages. Fry in 2 tablespoons oil for 7–8 minutes, turning once. Combine 200 g (7 oz) chickpeas with a bunch of coriander, chopped, 100 g (3½ oz) crumbled feta cheese, 2 tablespoons oil and 1 tablespoon lemon juice. Serve with the koftas.

Kofta-Inspired Skewers with

Chickpeas Crush 2 garlic cloves, and mix with 1 teaspoon ground cumin, 1 teaspoon ground coriander, ½ teaspoon ground cinnamon, a pinch of allspice (optional) and 1 tablespoon oil. Rub the mixture all over 500 g (1 lb) diced beef or lamb. Cut 1 onion and 1 green pepper into bite-sized pieces, then thread on to 8 short metal skewers with the meat. Place on a foil-lined grill rack and cook under a preheated grill for 6–8 minutes, turning occasionally, until cooked but tender. Cook 200 g (7 oz) long-grain rice in a saucepan of lightly salted boiling water for 12 minutes, until tender. Fold half a 400 g (13 oz) can chickpeas, drained and rinsed, and 1 small bunch of coriander, chopped, into the drained rice, and serve with the skewers, 100 g (3½ oz) crumbled feta cheese and ready-made tzatziki.

Mustard and Cheese Grilled Gammon

Serves 4

1 tablespoon vegetable oil

4 thick gammon steaks, about 175 g (6 oz) each

2 tablespoons wholegrain mustard

2 tablespoons chopped mixed herbs (such as parsley, chives, thyme and oregano)

75 g (3 oz) Cheddar cheese, grated

2 tablespoons onion chutney or 2 spring onions, finely sliced

To serve

crusty bread

mixed salad leaves

- Rub the oil over the gammon steaks and arrange on a foil-lined grill rack. Cook under a preheated grill for 4–5 minutes on each side, until cooked through.

- Meanwhile, mix the mustard with the chopped herbs, grated cheese and onion chutney or spring onions. Spoon the mixture on to the gammon steaks, return to the grill and cook under a moderate heat for a further 3–4 minutes, until melted and golden.

- Serve with crusty bread and mixed salad leaves.

---

10 Ham and Mustard Croque Monsieur

Mix 150 g (5 oz) coarsely grated Cheddar cheese in a bowl with 2 tablespoons mayonnaise, 1 tablespoon mustard and 2 tablespoons chopped mixed herbs (as above), then spread over 4 slices of sandwich bread. Top with 4 slices of cooked ham and cover each with a second piece of bread. Heat gently in a large nonstick frying pan for 6–7 minutes, turning once, until the bread is golden brown and the inside is hot and melted. Serve cut in half with salad leaves and onion chutney.

30 Cheese and Onion Grilled Gammon

Heat 2 tablespoons oil in a large nonstick frying pan and cook 4 thick gammon steaks, about 175 g (6 oz) each, for 6–7 minutes, turning once, until cooked and golden. Remove from the pan and set aside. Add 1 sliced onion to the pan and cook very gently for 10–12 minutes, until really soft and golden. Stir in 2 tablespoons chopped mixed herbs, 2 tablespoons wholegrain mustard and 200 ml (7 fl oz) low-salt vegetable stock, then simmer for 2–3 minutes to reduce slightly. Arrange the gammon steaks in a shallow ovenproof dish, then spoon the onion and herb mixture over the top, pouring over the juices. Top with 75 g (3 oz) grated Cheddar cheese and cook under a preheated grill for 3–4 minutes, until melted and golden. Serve with crusty bread, tomatoes and lettuce.

BUD-MEAT-FIQ

Pan-Fried Gnocchi and Chorizo Salad

Serves 4

2 tablespoons olive oil

400 g (13 oz) ready-made gnocchi

4 large, ripe tomatoes, roughly chopped

1 small bunch of basil leaves, roughly shredded

125 g (4 oz) mozzarella cheese, torn into pieces

100 g (3½ oz) sliced chorizo

1–2 tablespoons balsamic vinegar

salt and pepper

- Heat the olive oil in a large nonstick frying pan and add the gnocchi. Pan-fry for about 8 minutes, moving frequently, until crisp and golden.

- Meanwhile, toss the tomatoes with the basil leaves and torn mozzarella, season to taste and arrange on 4 serving plates.

- Add the chorizo to the pan of gnocchi for the final 1–2 minutes of cooking, until slightly crisp and golden. Scatter the gnocchi and chorizo over the salads, and serve drizzled with a little balsamic vinegar.

2 Pan-Fried Gnocchi with Chorizo and Tomato Sauce

Heat 2 tablespoons oil in a large nonstick frying pan and cook 1 chopped red onion for 7–8 minutes, until soft and golden. Chop 100 g (3½ oz) chorizo, add to the pan and cook for 1–2 minutes. Dice 4 large tomatoes and add to the pan with 1 tablespoon balsamic vinegar, and reduce the heat. Cook gently for 3–4 minutes, then stir in the leaves from a small bunch of basil, season to taste and remove from the heat. Meanwhile, fry 400 g (13 oz) ready-made gnocchi in a separate pan, following the main recipe. Spoon the gnocchi into 4 shallow bowls, then spoon over the chorizo and tomato sauce and serve scattered with 125 g (4 oz) mozzarella cheese, torn into pieces.

3 Creamy Gnocchi and Chorizo

Bake Dice 4 large tomatoes and place in a large bowl with 100 g (3½ oz) sliced chorizo, 750 g (1½ lb) ready-made gnocchi, 1 small bunch of basil leaves, roughly shredded, and 1–2 tablespoons balsamic vinegar. Season generously, then tip into a large ovenproof dish, pour over 140 ml (4½ fl oz) single cream and scatter with 125 g (4 oz) mozzarella cheese, torn into pieces. Cook in a preheated oven, 200°C (400°F), Gas Mark 6, for about 20 minutes until bubbling and golden. Serve with plenty of mixed salad leaves.

BUD-MEAT-VYK

 # Sesame Chicken and Noodles

Serves 4

350 g (11½ oz) skinless, boneless chicken breast or thigh, cut into thin strips

2 teaspoons cornflour

1 tablespoon dark soy sauce

1½ tablespoons sesame oil

2 teaspoons sesame seeds, plus extra to serve

2 teaspoons honey

2 tablespoons vegetable oil

1 onion, halved and thinly sliced

1 red pepper, cored, deseeded and thinly sliced

250 g (8 oz) courgettes, thinly sliced

1 tablespoon finely chopped fresh root ginger (optional)

400 g (13 oz) medium dried egg noodles

125 ml (4 fl oz) water

- Mix the chicken with the cornflour, soy sauce, 1 tablespoon of the sesame oil, sesame seeds and honey. Allow to marinate.

- Heat the vegetable oil in a large frying pan or wok, and fry the onion and red pepper for 3–4 minutes, until slightly softened. Add the courgettes and ginger, if using, and cook for a further 4–5 minutes, stirring frequently, until slightly softened.

- Meanwhile, bring a large saucepan of water to the boil, add the egg noodles and immediately remove from the heat. Cover and set aside for 4–5 minutes, until tender. Alternatively, cook according to packet instructions. Drain and refresh under cold water, then toss in the remaining sesame oil.

- Add the chicken and its marinade to the vegetables, and cook gently for 1–2 minutes to seal. Stir in the measured water and simmer gently for 2–3 minutes, until the chicken is cooked through and the sauce thickened.

- Add the noodles to the pan and cook for 1–2 minutes, until hot, then heap into bowls and serve sprinkled with extra sesame seeds.

---

10 Chicken Noodle Salad Cook and cool 400 g (13 oz) medium dried egg noodles, following the main recipe. Toss with 1 sliced red pepper, 2 sliced spring onions, 150 g (5 oz) bean sprouts and 250 g (8 oz) cooked chicken strips. Mix 2 tablespoons vegetable and 1½ tablespoons sesame oils, 2 teaspoons honey, 1 tablespoon dark soy sauce and 1 teaspoon finely grated fresh root ginger, and toss into the noodle salad. Serve sprinkled with sesame seeds.

30 Velvet Sesame Chicken Whisk 1 tablespoon cornflour and 1 egg white until foamy. Stir in 400 g (13 oz) cubed chicken breast and set aside at room temperature for at least 15 minutes. Drain the chicken on kitchen paper and pat dry. Heat 2 tablespoons vegetable oil in a large nonstick frying pan and cook the chicken for 3–4 minutes, until golden. Add 1 sliced yellow pepper and 1 sliced onion, and cook for a further 3–4 minutes, until beginning to soften. Add 250 g (8 oz) small broccoli florets and 1 tablespoon chopped fresh root ginger, and cook for 4–5 minutes, stirring frequently, until slightly softened. Then stir in 1½ tablespoons sesame oil, 2 teaspoons honey, 1 tablespoon dark soy sauce and 125 ml (4 fl oz) water, simmering gently for 2–3 minutes, until the chicken is completely cooked and the sauce thickened slightly. Spoon the chicken over bowls of hot, cooked noodles and sprinkle with sesame seeds to serve.

Ham and Mushroom Risotto

Serves 4

1.2 litres (2 pints) boiling ham or vegetable stock
15 g (½ oz) dried porcini mushrooms or mixed dried mushrooms (optional)
2 tablespoons olive oil
1 onion, chopped
1 garlic clove, chopped
200 g (7 oz) mushrooms, chopped
350 g (11½ oz) risotto rice
125 ml (4 fl oz) dry white wine
200 g (7 oz) piece of cooked ham off the bone, chopped
125 g (4 oz) mascarpone or cream cheese
salt and pepper
finely grated Parmesan-style cheese, to serve (optional)

- Pour the stock into a saucepan, add the dried mushrooms, if using, cover and simmer very gently for 8–10 minutes. If not using the dried mushrooms, pour the stock into the pan and keep at a gentle simmer.

- Heat the oil in a large frying pan and add the onion and garlic. Cook for 4–5 minutes, then add the chopped mushrooms and cook for a further 2–3 minutes, until softened. Add the rice and stir for a minute, until the grains are coated and translucent. Pour in the wine and simmer rapidly, stirring, until the liquid has been absorbed. Meanwhile, strain the dried mushrooms, if using, set aside and return the stock to the pan.

- Add the hot stock to the rice, a ladleful at a time, stirring constantly at a gentle simmer until each ladleful has been absorbed. Repeat this process until all of the stock has been absorbed and the rice is al dente. This should take 17 minutes.

- Chop the dried mushrooms, if using, and stir into the risotto with the ham and mascarpone and season generously. Stir to warm through, then remove from the heat, cover with a lid and set aside to rest for 2–3 minutes. Spoon the risotto into bowls, and serve with a little grated cheese, if desired.

---

1 Cheat's Ham and Mushroom Risotto

Heat 1 tablespoon oil in a frying pan, and cook 1 chopped onion and 1 chopped garlic clove for 4–5 minutes. Add 200 g (7 oz) chopped mushrooms and cook for 2 minutes more. Stir in 150 g (5 oz) chopped ham, 125 g (4 oz) mascarpone, 500 g (1 lb) ready-cooked rice and 200 ml (7 fl oz) hot vegetable stock. Stir until heated, season and serve.

2 Ham and Mushroom Fried

Rice Cook 350 g (11½ oz) quick-cook long-grain rice according to packet instructions, until just tender, then drain well. Heat 2 tablespoons vegetable oil in a large, deep-sided frying pan, and add 1 chopped onion and 1 chopped garlic clove. Cook for 4–5 minutes, then add 200 g (7 oz) chopped mushrooms and cook for a further 2–3 minutes, until softened. Add 2 tablespoons vegetable oil and the rice to the pan, with 150 g (5 oz) defrosted frozen peas and 200 g (7 oz) chopped cooked ham. Stir-fry for 3–4 minutes, stirring constantly, until lightly golden. Season with pepper and 2–3 teaspoons light soy sauce, and serve in shallow bowls.

Simple Sausage, Bean and Vegetable Stew

Serves 4

2 tablespoons vegetable oil

1 red onion, halved and sliced

2 garlic cloves, sliced

6 thick sausages, such as pork and sweet chilli

1 large red pepper, cored, deseeded and cut into quarters

400 g (13 oz) can chopped tomatoes

400 g (13 oz) can chickpeas or butter beans, drained and rinsed

2 teaspoons chopped rosemary, or 1 teaspoon dried rosemary

1 ham, vegetable or beef stock cube

200 ml (7 fl oz) hot water

steamed green vegetables, to serve (optional)

- Heat the oil in a deep-sided frying pan and cook the onion for 4 minutes. Add the garlic and cook for a further 1–2 minutes, until slightly softened.

- Meanwhile, arrange the sausages on a foil-lined grill rack with the red pepper pieces and cook under a preheated grill for 5–6 minutes, turning regularly, until browned. Cool slightly, then thickly slice the sausages diagonally and roughly chop the peppers.

- Pour the chopped tomatoes into the pan with the onions, then add the chickpeas or butter beans, rosemary, stock cube, measured water, the sausages and peppers. Cover with a lid, bring to the boil, then reduce the heat and simmer gently for 15–20 minutes, until thickened.

- Spoon the sausage and vegetable stew into 4 shallow bowls and serve with a selection of steamed green vegetables, if desired.

 Warm Chorizo and Bean Stew Heat 2 tablespoons oil in a frying pan, add 1 sliced red onion and cook for 4 minutes. Add 125 g (4 oz) diced chorizo and 2 sliced garlic cloves, and cook for a further 1–2 minutes. Meanwhile, quarter 1 red pepper and cook under a preheated grill for 5–6 minutes, turning. Mix 400 g (13 oz) can chickpeas with 3 diced tomatoes and 2 tablespoons chopped parsley. Season, then tip into the pan of chorizo and cook for 1–2 minutes. Spoon into 4 shallow dishes, top with the roasted peppers and serve.

 Grilled Sausages with Bean Stew Arrange 8 spicy sausages on a foil-lined grill rack and cook under a preheated grill for 16–18 minutes, turning occasionally, until cooked through, adding 1 red pepper, cut into quarters, for the final 5–6 minutes. Meanwhile, heat 2 tablespoons oil in a large nonstick frying pan, and cook 1 sliced red onion and 2 sliced garlic cloves for 4–5 minutes, until softened and lightly coloured. Add 400 g (13 oz) can chopped tomatoes, 400 g (13 oz) can chickpeas or butter beans, drained and rinsed, 2 teaspoons chopped rosemary, 1 stock cube and 200 ml (7 fl oz) hot water to the pan, then bring to the boil, reduce the heat and simmer gently for about 12–15 minutes, until thickened slightly. Spoon into bowls and serve with the grilled sausages and peppers.

 # Baked Aubergine with Lamb and Pine Nuts

Serves 4

5 tablespoons olive or
vegetable oil

2 aubergines, about 400 g (13 oz)
each, halved lengthways

1 onion, chopped

2 garlic cloves, sliced

25 g (1 oz) pine nuts

400 g (13 oz) minced lamb

2 teaspoons ground cumin

½ teaspoon ground cinnamon

3 tablespoons chopped mint

75 ml (3 fl oz) dry white wine

100 g (3½ oz) feta cheese

salt and pepper

To serve

steamed couscous

lemon wedges

- Preheat the oven to 200°C (400°F), Gas Mark 6. Heat 3 tablespoons of the oil in a large frying pan and cook the aubergines, cut sides down, for 5 minutes, until golden, then turn and cook the other sides for 2–3 minutes. Transfer them, cut sides up, to an ovenproof dish and season generously. Cook in the preheated oven for 8–10 minutes.

- Meanwhile, wipe the pan clean and heat the remaining oil in it. Add the onion and garlic, and cook for 5–6 minutes. Add the pine nuts and cook for 1–2 minutes, until golden.

- Add the minced lamb to the pan with the ground cumin and cinnamon, and fry over a medium-high heat, stirring frequently, for 5–6 minutes, until browned. Stir in the chopped mint and season lightly.

- Remove the aubergines from the oven, spoon the lamb mixture over the top and pour over the white wine. Crumble over the feta and return to the oven for a further 10–15 minutes, until bubbling and lightly golden. Serve with lemon wedges and steamed couscous.

 ### Griddled Lamb with Pine Nuts

Mix 5 tablespoons olive oil with 2 teaspoons ground cumin, ½ teaspoon ground cinnamon, grated rind of 1 lemon, and salt and pepper, and rub into 4 lamb leg steaks. Heat a griddle pan and cook the steaks for 3–4 minutes on each side. Scatter with 25 g (1 oz) pine nuts, 3 tablespoons chopped mint and 100 g (3½ oz) crumbled feta cheese, and serve with couscous and lemon wedges.

 ### Lamb, Aubergine and Pine Nut

Burgers Place 400 g (13 oz) minced lamb in a bowl with 50 g (2 oz) fresh breadcrumbs, 1 finely chopped onion, 1 crushed garlic clove, 1 tablespoon pine nuts, 1 beaten egg, 2 teaspoons ground cumin, ½ teaspoon ground cinnamon, 3 tablespoons chopped mint and seasoning. Mix well and form into 4 burgers. Heat 1 tablespoon oil in a nonstick frying pan and cook the burgers for 4–5 minutes each side, until browned and cooked through. Meanwhile, cut 1 aubergine into 5-mm (¼-inch) slices and cook on a preheated ridged griddle pan for 7–8 minutes, turning occasionally, until charred and softened. Remove from the heat, drizzle with 1 tablespoon oil and season with salt and pepper. Griddle the cut sides of 4 split bread rolls, and serve the burgers in the rolls in between slices of griddled aubergine and 100 g (3½ oz) sliced feta cheese.

QuickCook
Fish and Seafood

Recipes listed by cooking time

30

20

10

Tuna Rissoles with Coriander Mayonnaise

Serves 4

4–5 spring onions, chopped
1 garlic clove, roughly chopped
1.5-cm (¾-inch) piece of fresh
   root ginger, peeled and chopped
1 red chilli, deseeded and chopped
3 tablespoons vegetable oil
2 x 200 g (7 oz) cans tuna, drained
50 g (2 oz) cooked white rice
50 g (2 oz) fresh breadcrumbs
2 tablespoons sweet chilli sauce
1 egg, lightly beaten
1 tablespoon chopped coriander
2–3 tablespoons plain flour
handful of rocket, to garnish

For the coriander mayonnaise

3 tablespoons mayonnaise
1 tablespoon chopped coriander
2 teaspoons lime or lemon juice
salt and pepper

- Place the spring onions in a mini-chopper or the small bowl of a food processor with the garlic, ginger and chilli, and pulse briefly, until finely chopped. Alternatively, chop finely by hand. Heat 1 tablespoon of the oil in a small frying pan and cook the mixture for 2–3 minutes, until aromatic and slightly softened. Set aside to cool slightly.

- Meanwhile, place the tuna in a large bowl with the rice, breadcrumbs, chilli sauce, egg and coriander. Add the cooked onion mixture and mix gently to combine. Shape into 12 rissoles, cover and chill in the refrigerator for about 12 minutes.

- To make the coriander mayonnaise, spoon the mayonnaise into a small bowl, stir in the coriander and the lime or lemon juice. Season to taste and set aside.

- Heat the remaining oil in a large nonstick frying pan. Dust the rissoles lightly in the flour and fry for 6–7 minutes, turning occasionally, until crisp and golden. Serve the rissoles hot with the coriander mayonnaise and garnish with rocket leaves.

Zesty Tuna Rice Salad Peel and grate a 1.5-cm (¾-inch) piece of fresh root ginger, crush 1 small garlic clove, deseed and finely chop 1 red chilli, then place in a bowl with 3 tablespoons vegetable oil and 2 tablespoons lime juice. Whisk to combine. In a large bowl, mix 500 g (1 lb) cooked rice with 4–5 finely sliced spring onions, 1 finely chopped red pepper and 2 x 200 g (7 oz) cans tuna, drained and flaked. Fold in the dressing and serve immediately.

Spicy Fresh Tuna Burgers Place 300 g (10 oz) raw tuna in a food processor with 1 teaspoon Thai red curry paste and 2 tablespoons chopped fresh coriander, and pulse briefly, until finely chopped. Transfer to a bowl and mix gently with 1 small beaten egg, 2 finely chopped spring onions, 50 g (2 oz) cooked white rice and 50 g (2 oz) fresh breadcrumbs, then form into 4 burgers. Heat 3 tablespoons vegetable oil in a large nonstick frying pan and cook the burgers for 2–3 minutes each side, until just cooked and golden. Serve in toasted buns with the coriander mayonnaise from the main recipe and some salad leaves.

BUD-FISH-BUY

Prawn, Avocado and Coriander Tostada

Serves 4

4 large soft flour tortillas
1 small iceberg lettuce, shredded
300 g (10 oz) cooked peeled
  prawns
1 large, ripe but firm avocado,
  peeled and diced
2 tablespoons chopped fresh
  coriander
1 tablespoon lime juice
salt and cracked black pepper
lime wedges, to serve

- Heat a griddle pan and toast a tortilla for 30–60 seconds on each side, until lightly charred. Immediately push it into a small, deep bowl and set aside. Repeat with the remaining tortillas to make 4 bowl-shaped tortillas. Place one-quarter of the shredded lettuce inside each one.

- Meanwhile, toss together the prawns, avocado, coriander and lime juice, and season to taste. Divide between the tortillas and serve with the lime wedges.

Prawn and Black Bean Chilli Heat 2 tablespoons vegetable oil in a large frying pan, and add 4 chopped spring onions, 2 chopped garlic cloves and 1 finely chopped and deseeded red chilli. Cook gently for 2 minutes, until softened, then add a 400 g (13 oz) can chopped tomatoes, and a 400 g (13 oz) can black beans, drained and rinsed. Simmer gently for 10–12 minutes, until thickened slightly. Stir in 3 tablespoons chopped coriander, 1 tablespoon lime juice and 250 g (8 oz) cooked peeled prawns. Simmer for 1 minute, until the prawns are hot, and serve with griddled tortillas and lime wedges, scattered with extra coriander.

Mexican Prawn Rice with Avocado Salad Heat 2 tablespoons vegetable oil in a large saucepan or casserole, and gently cook 4 chopped spring onions, 2 chopped garlic cloves and 1 finely chopped and deseeded red chilli for 2 minutes. Stir 250 g (8 oz) long-grain rice and a 30 g (1¼ oz) sachet of mild fajita spice mix into the pan, then add a 400 g (13 oz) can of chopped tomatoes and 575 ml (18 fl oz) hot vegetable stock. Stir to combine, then bring to the boil, reduce the heat and cover with a tight-fitting lid. Simmer gently for 20–25 minutes, until the rice is tender, adding 200 g (7 oz) cooked peeled prawns for the last minute. Meanwhile, toss 1 peeled and diced avocado gently with 1 tablespoon lime juice and 2 tablespoons chopped fresh coriander. Serve the rice in bowls topped with a spoonful of avocado salad and griddled tortillas.

Smoked Mackerel Brandade

Serves 4

750 g (1½ lb) floury potatoes, peeled and cut into chunks
500–750 ml (17 fl oz–1¼ pints) hot milk
2 garlic cloves, sliced
150 g (5 oz) smoked mackerel fillets, skin removed
150 ml (¼ pint) crème fraîche
3 tablespoons chopped parsley
4 tablespoons olive oil
salt and pepper
hot toast, to serve

• Place the potatoes in a medium saucepan and pour over enough milk to cover. Add the sliced garlic and a little seasoning, then bring to the boil and cook for about 15 minutes, or until tender.

• Meanwhile, place the smoked mackerel in the small bowl of a food processor with the crème fraîche, and blend until smooth. Stir in the chopped parsley and plenty of cracked black pepper.

• Drain the potatoes, reserving the milk. Return the potatoes to the pan with 4 tablespoons of the milk and the olive oil, and mash until smooth. Mix in the mackerel and season to taste with salt and pepper. Spoon into 4 small bowls and serve immediately with plenty of hot toast.

---

10 **Smoked Mackerel Pâté** Place 150 g (5 oz) smoked mackerel in a food processor with 150 g (5 oz) cream cheese, 1 tablespoon creamed horseradish, 2 teaspoons lemon juice and 3 tablespoons chopped parsley. Blend until almost smooth, then season to taste with salt and pepper. Serve the pâté accompanied by plenty of hot toast.

30 **Hot Mackerel Brandade Bake** Place 750 g (1½ lb) floury potatoes, peeled and cut into chunks, in a medium saucepan and pour over enough milk to cover. Add 2 sliced garlic cloves and a little seasoning, then bring to the boil and cook for about 10 minutes, until just tender but still firm. Drain and tip into a large ovenproof dish. Sprinkle with 150 g (5 oz) flaked smoked mackerel fillets. Mix 3 tablespoons chopped parsley with 400 ml (14 fl oz) crème fraîche, season to taste and pour over the potatoes. Sprinkle with 150 g (5 oz) Emmental or Cheddar and cook in a preheated oven, 200°C (400°F), Gas Mark 6, for 15–20 minutes until bubbling and golden. Serve with a green salad.

30 Easy Fish Pie with Crunchy Potato Topping

Serves 4

750 g (1½ lb) medium potatoes, unpeeled

250 g (8 oz) white fish fillet, such as coley, pollack or haddock, cut into bite-sized pieces

250 g (8 oz) salmon fillet, cut into bite-sized pieces

400 ml (14 fl oz) hot milk

50 g (2 oz) butter

50 g (2 oz) flour

100 g (3½ oz) Cheddar cheese, grated

2 teaspoons lemon juice

2 tablespoons chopped chives

100 g (3½ oz) small cooked peeled prawns (optional)

salt and pepper

- Preheat the oven to 180°C (350°F), Gas Mark 4. Cook the potatoes in a large saucepan of lightly salted water for 6–7 minutes. Drain and set aside to cool slightly.

- Meanwhile, place the fish in a deep-sided frying pan. Pour over the hot milk and bring to the boil. Reduce the heat and simmer gently for 3–4 minutes, until the fish is just cooked. Strain the milk into a jug and transfer the fish to an ovenproof dish.

- Place the butter and flour in a saucepan and warm gently to melt the butter. Stir over the heat to cook the flour for 2 minutes, then add the milk a little at a time, stirring well to incorporate. Stir over the heat for 2–3 minutes, until thickened, then remove from the heat and stir in half the cheese, the lemon juice and chives, and season to taste. Pour the sauce over the fish, add the prawns, if using, and stir gently to coat.

- Wearing rubber gloves to protect your hands from the heat, grate the potatoes coarsely and scatter over the fish. Sprinkle with the remaining cheese and cook in the preheated oven for 15–20 minutes, until the topping is golden and crispy.

---

1 **Easy Fried Fish**
Heat 2 tablespoons oil in a large nonstick frying pan and cook 4 chunky salmon or white fish fillets, approximately 150 g (5 oz) each, for about 3 minutes on each side, until just cooked. Season generously. Serve on warmed plates with 1 kg (2 lb) ready-made mashed potatoes and drizzled with 350 g (11½ oz) ready-made cheese sauce.

2 **Easy Baked Fish**
Place 4 chunky salmon or white fish fillets, approximately 150 g (5 oz) each, on a greased baking sheet. In a bowl, mix 50 g (2 oz) fresh breadcrumbs with the grated rind of 1 lemon, 2 tablespoons chopped chives, 1 tablespoon olive oil and some seasoning. Pile the breadcrumb mixture on top of the fish fillets and cook in a preheated oven, 200°C (400°F),

Gas Mark 6, for 12–15 minutes, until the fish is cooked and the topping golden. Meanwhile, cook 1 kg (2 lb) peeled potatoes, cut into small chunks, in a large saucepan of lightly salted boiling water for about 15 minutes, until tender. Mash until smooth with 50 g (2 oz) butter, 1 tablespoon lemon juice and 75 ml (3 fl oz) double cream or milk. Season to taste and serve topped with the crunchy fish fillets.

Tomato, Mussel and Aubergine Shells

Serves 4

4 tablespoons olive or
  vegetable oil
2 garlic cloves, chopped
1 large onion, finely chopped
1 red chilli, deseeded and finely
  chopped
400 g (13 oz) can chopped
  tomatoes
100 ml (3½ fl oz) water
1 teaspoon finely grated
  lemon rind
pinch of sugar
400 g (13 oz) pasta shells
1 aubergine, diced
200 g (7 oz) cooked shelled
  mussels

- Heat half the oil in a saucepan, add the chopped garlic, onion and chilli, and cook for 1–2 minutes, until just softened. Add the tomatoes, measured water, lemon rind and sugar, then season to taste and simmer gently for 15–18 minutes.

- Cook the pasta shells in a large saucepan of lightly salted boiling water for 11 minutes, or according to packet instructions, until al dente.

- Meanwhile, heat the remaining oil in a large frying pan and cook the aubergine for about 8 minutes, turning occasionally, until golden. Transfer to the simmering pan of tomato sauce for the remaining cooking time.

- Stir the mussels into the tomato sauce for the final minute, cook until thoroughly heated through, then spoon over the drained pasta to serve.

10 Tomato and Mussel Fusilli

Cook 400 g (13 oz) quick-cook fusilli pasta according to packet instructions. Heat 4 tablespoons olive or vegetable oil in a pan, add 2 chopped garlic cloves and 1 deseeded and finely chopped red chilli, and cook for 1–2 minutes. Add 300 g (10 oz) defrosted frozen mussels, cook for 1 minute, then stir in 4 diced tomatoes, 1 teaspoon finely grated lemon rind and 1 tablespoon lemon juice. Season generously to taste, then toss immediately with the drained pasta and spoon into bowls to serve.

30 Cheesy Baked Mussel and Aubergine Pasta

Make the mussel and aubergine sauce following the main recipe. Cook 400 g (13 oz) fusilli or penne pasta according to packet instructions, until al dente, then drain. Toss with the pasta sauce and transfer to a large ovenproof dish. Arrange 200 g (7 oz) thinly sliced mozzarella over the top and drizzle with 1 tablespoon oil. Cook under a preheated grill for 6–7 minutes, until lightly golden and melted. Serve with a rocket salad.

BUD-FISH-KUK

Frying-Pan Pizza with Anchovies

Serves 4

300 g (10 oz) self-raising flour,
  plus extra for dusting
1 teaspoon dried thyme
150 ml (¼ pint) warm water
1½ tablespoons olive oil
6 tablespoons ready-made pizza
  or tomato pasta sauce
50 g (2 oz) can anchovies, drained
2 tablespoons capers, drained
  and rinsed
125 g (4 oz) mozzarella cheese,
  diced
salt and pepper

- Mix the flour in a bowl with the thyme and a generous pinch of salt and pepper. Pour in the warm water and olive oil, and mix to form a soft dough.

- Divide the dough in half and roll out on a lightly floured surface to fit 2 large nonstick frying pans, approximately 28 cm (11 inches) across. Dust with a little flour. Heat the frying pans over a medium heat and lower the circles of dough carefully into the pans. Cook for about 10 minutes, turning once, until lightly golden.

- Spread the sauce over the pizza bases and scatter with anchovies and capers. Sprinkle over the mozzarella and cook under a preheated grill for 3–5 minutes, until golden and bubbling. Serve immediately.

10 Anchovy and Black Olive Tapenade

Place 100 g (3½ oz) pitted black olives in a mini-chopper or the small bowl of a food processor with 6 drained anchovy fillets, 2 tablespoons drained and rinsed capers, 1 crushed garlic clove and ½ teaspoon dried thyme. Blend to a smooth paste and stir in 2 tablespoons oil and 1 teaspoon lemon juice. Spread the tapenade over slices of French bread and serve topped with mozzarella.

30 Mini Tuna and Anchovy Pizzas

Make the dough following the main recipe, then divide into approximately 16 small balls. Roll out each ball thinly and arrange on 2 lightly floured baking sheets. Cook in a preheated oven, 200°C (400°F), Gas Mark 6, for 3–4 minutes until lightly golden. Spread 6 tablespoons ready-made pizza or tomato pasta sauce on the mini pizzas, then drain a 200 g (7 oz) can tuna and divide between them.

Top each one with 1 chopped anchovy fillet and a little mozzarella, then return to the oven for 8–10 minutes, until the pizzas are crisp and melting. Serve hot with a lamb's lettuce salad.

BUD-FISH-MYI

Teriyaki Salmon Sticks with Bean Sprout Salad

Serves 4

500 g (1 lb) skinless, boneless salmon fillet, cut into bite-sized pieces

100 ml (3½ fl oz) teriyaki marinade

1 tablespoon sesame or vegetable oil, plus extra for greasing

200 g (7 oz) bean sprouts

2 carrots, peeled and coarsely grated

2 spring onions, chopped

3 tablespoons roughly chopped coriander

1 tablespoon rice wine vinegar or white wine vinegar

- Place the salmon in a bowl with three-quarters of the teriyaki marinade. Mix to coat and set aside for 10 minutes. Lightly grease a baking sheet.

- Meanwhile, mix the bean sprouts, carrots, spring onions and coriander in a large bowl. Combine the remaining teriyaki marinade with the vegetable oil and vinegar in a small bowl to make a dressing.

- Thread the salmon pieces on to 4 metal skewers and arrange on the greased baking sheet. Cook under a preheated grill for about 8 minutes, turning occasionally, until almost cooked through.

- Toss the salad with the dressing and arrange on 4 plates, then serve with the hot salmon skewers.

Smoked Salmon and Teriyaki Salad

Mix 200 g (7 oz) bean sprouts, 2 coarsely grated carrots, 2 chopped spring onions and 3 tablespoons chopped coriander in a large bowl. Combine 25 ml (1 fl oz) teriyaki marinade with 1 tablespoon sesame oil and 1 tablespoon rice wine vinegar to make a dressing. Slice 200 g (7 oz) smoked salmon or smoked salmon trimmings into strips. Divide the salad between 4 plates, scatter over the smoked salmon and drizzle with the dressing, to serve.

Teriyaki Salmon Parcels

Cut 500 g (1 lb) skinless, boneless salmon fillet into 4 pieces and place in a shallow dish. Combine 100 ml (3½ fl oz) teriyaki marinade with 1 tablespoon sesame oil and 1 tablespoon rice wine vinegar, pour over the salmon, mix to coat and set aside for 10 minutes. Meanwhile, cut 2 carrots and 2 spring onions into thin matchsticks, and thinly shred half a Chinese cabbage. Toss the vegetables in a large bowl with 200 g (7 oz) bean sprouts and 3 tablespoons roughly chopped coriander, then divide between 4 large squares of foil. Top each pile of vegetables with a salmon fillet, then drizzle over any leftover marinade. Fold up the sides of the foil and scrunch together to make 4 parcels. Place on a baking sheet and cook in a preheated oven, 200°C (400°F), Gas Mark 6, for 12–15 minutes, until the salmon is just cooked through and the vegetables have softened. Serve with a bowl of steamed rice, if desired.

BUD-FISH-MEB

Thai-Flavoured Mussels with Coconut Milk

Serves 4

2 tablespoons vegetable oil
2 shallots, halved and finely sliced
2.5-cm (1-inch) piece of fresh
  root ginger, peeled and
  finely chopped
1 garlic clove, finely sliced
1 green chilli, deseeded and
  finely sliced
200 ml (7 fl oz) coconut milk
2 teaspoons Thai fish sauce
300 ml (½ pint) vegetable stock
1 kg (2 lb) mussels, scrubbed, and
  any unopened shells discarded
1 small bunch of coriander,
  roughly chopped, to garnish
  (optional)

- Heat the oil in a large saucepan or casserole, and cook the shallots, ginger, garlic and chilli gently for 6–8 minutes, until really soft.

- Add the coconut milk, fish sauce and stock, and heat to boiling point. Simmer gently for 5–6 minutes to allow the flavours to develop, then stir in the mussels. Cover with a tight-fitting lid and leave to cook gently for 4–5 minutes, shaking the pan occasionally, until all the mussels have opened, discarding any that remain closed.

- Spoon into large, shallow bowls with the coconut-flavoured soup and serve immediately scattered with coriander, if using.

---

1 **Thai Green Curry Mussels** Heat 2 tablespoons vegetable oil in a large casserole or saucepan, and add 2 tablespoons Thai green curry paste. Pour in 200 ml (7 fl oz) coconut milk and 300 ml (½ pint) hot vegetable stock, bring to the boil and add 1 kg (2 lb) scrubbed mussels. Cover and cook gently for 4–5 minutes, shaking the pan occasionally, until all the mussels have opened. Serve immediately, scattered with chopped coriander, if desired.

3 **Thai-Flavoured Mussel and Noodle Soup** In a large pan, heat 1 litre (1¾ pints) chicken or vegetable stock with 3 tablespoons fish sauce, 1 tablespoon light brown sugar, the finely chopped stalks from a bunch of coriander, 2 finely sliced shallots, 1 finely sliced garlic clove, a peeled and finely chopped 2.5-cm (1-inch) piece of fresh root ginger and 1 deseeded and finely sliced green chilli. Simmer gently for about 20 minutes to allow the flavours to develop. Meanwhile, cook 300 g (10 oz) straight-to-wok rice noodles according to packet instructions, and divide between 4 deep, warmed bowls. Strain the soup through a sieve and return to the pan with 200 ml (7 fl oz) coconut milk and 200 g (7 oz) cooked shelled mussels. Heat for 1–2 minutes, until the mussels are hot, then stir in 2 tablespoons lime juice and ladle over the bowls of noodles. Serve immediately, scattered with the chopped coriander leaves.

10 Chilli and Anchovy Dressed Pasta

Serves 4

400 g (13 oz) quick-cook
  spaghetti
3 tablespoons olive oil
2 garlic cloves, chopped
1 red chilli, deseeded and
  finely sliced
2 tablespoons lemon juice
3 tablespoons chopped flat
  leaf parsley
50 g (2 oz) anchovy fillets in oil,
  drained and roughly chopped
pepper

- Cook the spaghetti in a large saucepan of lightly salted boiling water for 4–5 minutes, or according to packet instructions, until al dente.

- Meanwhile, heat the olive oil in a small pan and add the garlic and chilli. Simmer gently in the oil for 2 minutes, until softened, then remove from the heat.

- Drain the pasta and toss immediately with the garlic and chilli oil, lemon juice, parsley and chopped anchovies. Season to taste with pepper and serve in warmed bowls.

20 Chilli and Anchovy Griddled Fish

Place 4 chunky, skinless, boneless white fish fillets on a board and top each with 2 anchovy fillets. Sprinkle with 3 tablespoons chopped parsley, 1 deseeded, sliced red chilli and the finely grated rind of 1 lemon. Wrap each fillet in a large slice of Parma-style ham and drizzle with 1 tablespoon olive oil. Heat a griddle pan and cook the parcels for 7–8 minutes, turning occasionally, until just cooked through. Meanwhile, cook 400 g (13 oz) quick-cook spaghetti according to packet instructions. Drain, and toss in 2 tablespoons olive oil and 2 tablespoons lemon juice. Season to taste with salt and pepper. Heap into 4 warmed bowls and top each with a griddled cod and anchovy parcel.

30 Chilli, Anchovy and Red Pepper Pasta

Cut 3 red peppers in half and arrange them, cut side up, in a large roasting tin. Fill each pepper half with 2 cherry tomatoes, a little chopped garlic, 1 anchovy fillet and a scattering of chopped red chilli. Drizzle with 3 tablespoons olive oil and 2 tablespoons lemon juice, and cook in a preheated oven, 200°C (400°F), Gas Mark 6, for 20 minutes until slightly softened. Meanwhile, cook 400 g (13 oz) spaghetti in a large saucepan of lightly salted boiling water for 11 minutes, or according to packet instructions, until al dente. Tip the filled roasted peppers into a food processor, pulse briefly to make a roughly chopped sauce and toss quickly with the drained pasta. Heap into bowls and serve immediately, scattered with chopped parsley.

Salmon Fishcakes with Tartare Sauce

Serves 4

300 g (10 oz) potatoes, peeled and cut into chunks

2 x 175 g (6 oz) cans salmon, drained

2 tablespoons chopped mixed herbs (such as chives, tarragon and parsley)

25 g (1 oz) gherkins, finely chopped

1 tablespoon capers, rinsed and finely chopped

50 g (2 oz) plain flour

1 large egg, lightly beaten

75 g (3 oz) fresh breadcrumbs

oil, for shallow frying

salt and pepper

handful of rocket, to garnish

For the tartare sauce

6 tablespoons mayonnaise

1 tablespoon lemon juice

1 tablespoon capers, rinsed and finely chopped

25 g (1 oz) gherkins, chopped

- Cook the potatoes in a large saucepan of lightly salted boiling water for about 12 minutes, until tender. Drain well, mash until almost smooth, then allow to cool slightly.

- Meanwhile, flake the salmon into a bowl and add the herbs, gherkins and capers. Season generously with salt and pepper, then mix gently with the potatoes and form into 8 fishcakes. Dust in the flour, dip both sides in the beaten egg to coat, then turn in the breadcrumbs to cover. Cover loosely with clingfilm and chill for about 10 minutes.

- Meanwhile, make the tartare sauce by combining all the ingredients together in a bowl. Season with salt and pepper and set aside.

- Heat the oil in a large nonstick frying pan and cook the fishcakes for 2–3 minutes each side, until crisp and golden. Garnish with rocket leaves and serve with the tartare sauce.

Smoked Salmon Rillettes Place 250 g (8 oz) smoked salmon trimmings in a food processor with 2 tablespoons chopped fresh herbs, 2 teaspoons lemon juice, 1 tablespoon chopped gherkins and 1 teaspoon drained and rinsed capers, and pulse until finely chopped. Add 150 g (5 oz) cream cheese and some black pepper, and blend until almost smooth. Scrape into 4 small ramekins and serve with crispbreads.

Baked Salmon with Capers Mix 2 tablespoons chopped fresh mixed herbs in a small bowl with 1 tablespoon capers, 1 tablespoon finely chopped gherkins and 125 g (4 oz) cream cheese. Place 4 chunky salmon fillets, about 150 g (5 oz) each, in an ovenproof dish and cut a pocket down the middle of each one. Open up the pockets and stuff with the cream cheese mixture. Season and cook in a preheated oven, 200°C (400°F), Gas Mark 6, for 12–15 minutes until the salmon is cooked through. Meanwhile, cook 1 kg (2 lb) peeled potatoes in a saucepan of lightly salted boiling water for 12–15 minutes, until tender. Drain and mash until smooth with 50 g (2 oz) butter and 50 ml (2 fl oz) single cream. Spoon the mash on to 4 plates, top with the cooked salmon fillets and squeeze over a little lemon juice. Serve immediately with ready-made tartare sauce.

30 Golden Pollack with Homemade Chips and Herby Peas

Serves 4

1 kg (2 lb) large potatoes, peeled
  and cut into thick fingers
3 tablespoons vegetable oil
25 g (1 oz) butter
2 shallots, chopped
300 g (10 oz) frozen peas
3 tablespoons chopped mixed
  herbs (such as parsley,
  mint and chives)
50 ml (2 fl oz) hot vegetable
  stock
olive oil, for shallow frying
4 pollack fillets, approximately
  125 g (4 oz) each
salt and pepper

- Preheat the oven to 200°C (400°F), Gas Mark 6. Cook the potato chips in a large saucepan of lightly salted boiling water for 3 minutes. Drain well and pat dry with a dry tea towel. Toss the chips in a large bowl with the vegetable oil and a little salt and pepper. Tip on to a large baking sheet and cook in the preheated oven for 20–25 minutes, turning occasionally, until tender and golden.

- Meanwhile, heat the butter in a medium-sized saucepan and cook the shallots for 6–7 minutes, until softened. Add the peas, chopped herbs and the vegetable stock, and season to taste with salt and pepper. Cover and simmer gently for 3–4 minutes, until the peas are tender, then remove from the heat and keep warm.

- Heat the olive oil in a nonstick frying pan. Season the pollack fillets with a little salt and pepper, then fry gently for about 3 minutes on each side, until golden and only just cooked through. Serve the fish with the chips and herby peas.

10 Pan-Fried Pollack with Herby Pea

Purée Cook 500 g (1 lb) frozen peas in a saucepan of boiling water for 2–3 minutes, until tender. Drain and tip into a food processor with 50 g (2 oz) butter and 3 tablespoons chopped fresh herbs. Blend until smooth, then transfer back to the pan and keep warm. Meanwhile, season 4 pollack fillets and pan-fry in a little olive oil for about 3 minutes on each side, until golden. Spoon the herby pea purée on to 4 warmed plates and serve with the pollack and lemon wedges.

20 Roast Pollack with Mushy Peas

Arrange 750 g (1½ lb) frozen oven chips on a large baking sheet and cook in a preheated oven, 220°C (425°F), Gas Mark 7, for 15–20 minutes, or according to packet instructions, until tender and golden. Meanwhile, place 4 pollack fillets skin side down on a lightly greased baking tray, drizzle with olive oil and season generously with salt and pepper. Roast in the oven for about 10 minutes, until just cooked. While the chips and fish are in the oven, heat 25 g (1 oz) butter in a medium-sized saucepan and cook 2 chopped shallots for 6–7 minutes, until softened. Add 300 g (10 oz) frozen peas, 3 tablespoons chopped fresh mixed herbs and 50 ml (2 fl oz) hot vegetable stock. Cover and simmer gently for 3–4 minutes, then drain off the liquid and tip the peas into a food processor. Blend until just mushy, then return to the pan, season to taste and keep warm. Serve the roast pollack on warmed plates with the braised pea purée and oven chips.

Blackened Sardines with Yogurt Dressing

Serves 4

12–16 fresh sardines, gutted and scaled

2 teaspoons paprika

1 teaspoon dried oregano

½ teaspoon ground cayenne pepper

½ teaspoon dried garlic powder

2 tablespoons olive or vegetable oil

150 ml (¼ pint) plain yogurt

2 tablespoons chopped chives

2 tablespoons lime or lemon juice

salt and pepper

- Use a sharp knife to make 3 slashes in each side of each sardine. Mix the paprika, oregano, cayenne pepper, garlic powder and oil, season with salt and pepper, and massage all over the sardines. Set aside to marinate for 8–10 minutes.

- Meanwhile, mix the yogurt with the chives and lime or lemon juice, and season to taste. Set aside.

- Arrange the sardines on a grill rack and cook under a preheated grill for 5–6 minutes, turning once, until slightly blackened and cooked through. Serve with the yogurt dressing.

Sardine and Rice Salad with Yogurt Dressing Drain and flake 400 g (13 oz) canned sardine fillets, and toss with 500 g (1 lb) cold cooked rice, 1 finely chopped red pepper and the diced flesh of 1 avocado. Combine 150 ml (¼ pint) plain yogurt with 2 tablespoons chopped chives and 2 tablespoons lime or lemon juice, and season to taste. Drizzle the yogurt dressing over the salad before serving.

Cajun Sardines with Rice Heat 2 tablespoons olive or vegetable oil in a large nonstick frying pan, and add 1 chopped red pepper, 1 chopped red onion and 2 chopped garlic cloves. Cook for 8–9 minutes, or until soft and golden. Add 1 teaspoon dried oregano, ½ teaspoon ground cayenne pepper and ½ teaspoon dried garlic powder, and cook for 1 minute before adding a 400 g (13 oz) can chopped tomatoes, 3 chopped anchovy fillets in oil and 200 ml (7 fl oz) water. Season and simmer gently for about 15 minutes, until thickened. Meanwhile, cook 250 g (8 oz) long-grain rice in a large saucepan of lightly salted boiling water for about 12 minutes, or according to packet instructions, until just tender. Stir 400 g (13 oz) canned sardine fillets, drained and flaked, into the tomato sauce, heat for 1 minute and serve spooned over the cooked rice.

BUD-FISH-GAN

Creamy Mustard and Trout Pasta Salad

Serves 4

1 tablespoon light olive oil
4 skinless, boneless trout fillets, approximately 100 g (3½ oz) each, seasoned lightly
400 g (13 oz) pasta shells
12 cherry tomatoes, halved
½ cucumber, diced

For the dressing

50 g (2 oz) mayonnaise
2 tablespoons lemon juice
3 anchovy fillets in oil, drained and roughly chopped
1 small garlic clove
1 teaspoon sugar
3 tablespoons grated Parmesan-style cheese
1 tablespoon wholegrain mustard
100 ml (3½ fl oz) light olive or groundnut oil
salt and pepper

- Heat the oil in a nonstick frying pan and pan-fry the trout fillets for 4–5 minutes, turning once, until just cooked through but still slightly pink in the middle. Remove from the pan and set aside to cool a little.

- Cook the pasta in a large saucepan of lightly salted boiling water for 11 minutes, or according to packet instructions, until al dente. Drain well, refresh under cold running water and drain again.

- Meanwhile, place the dressing ingredients, except the mustard and oil, in a small food processor and blend until smooth. Transfer to a bowl and slowly whisk in the mustard and oil. Season to taste.

- Flake the trout into large pieces and toss with the pasta, cherry tomatoes and cucumber. Spoon into bowls, then drizzle over the mustard dressing and serve immediately.

Trout and Pasta Caesar Salad

Cook 400 g (13 oz) quick-cook penne pasta according to packet instructions, cool under running water, then drain well and tip into a large bowl. Flake 250 g (8 oz) ready-cooked trout or salmon fillets into the pasta and add ½ diced cucumber, 12 halved cherry tomatoes and 8 tablespoons ready-made Caesar dressing. Mix, then spoon into 4 bowls and serve scattered with 100 g (3½ oz) ready-made croûtons, if desired.

Filo-Topped Creamy Mustard Trout Fillets

Place 4 chunky trout fillets in a snug-fitting ovenproof dish. Mix 1 tablespoon wholegrain mustard with 150 g (5 oz) cream cheese, and spread in a thick layer over the fish. Drizzle with 150 ml (¼ pint) double cream and 1 tablespoon lemon juice. Brush 4 filo pastry sheets, approximately 23 x 25 cm (9 x 10 inches), with 25 g (1 oz) melted butter and scrunch up the pastry slightly before placing one sheet on top of each fillet. Cook in a preheated oven, 180°C (350°F), Gas Mark 4, for 18–20 minutes, until the fish is just cooked and the pastry crisp and golden. Make the dressing following the main recipe. Serve the fish on a bed of tagliatelle pasta, drizzled with the creamy mustard sauce.

30 Chilli Crab and Rice Cakes with Lime Dipping Sauce

Serves 4

2 x 175 g (6 oz) cans crab meat
3 spring onions, chopped
100 g (3½ oz) cooked rice
75 g (3 oz) dried breadcrumbs
1 red chilli, deseeded and chopped
3 tablespoons chopped coriander
finely grated rind of ½ lime
2 small eggs, lightly beaten
1 teaspoon Thai fish sauce
vegetable oil, for shallow frying
lime wedges, to serve

For the dipping sauce

4 tablespoons caster sugar
2 tablespoons rice wine vinegar
  or white wine vinegar
2 tablespoons water
finely grated rind of ½ lime
1 tablespoon lime juice
2 teaspoons Thai fish sauce
½ red chilli, deseeded and chopped

- In a large bowl, mix the crab meat, spring onions, rice, breadcrumbs, chilli, coriander and half of the lime rind. Add the beaten egg and fish sauce to the bowl, and mix to combine, adding extra breadcrumbs if the mixture seems a little damp.

- Form the mixture into 12 crab cakes, then arrange on a plate, cover lightly and chill in the refrigerator for 10–12 minutes to firm up.

- Meanwhile, make the dipping sauce. Place the caster sugar, vinegar and measured water in a small pan, and warm over a low heat until the sugar dissolves. Stir in the lime rind and juice, fish sauce and chilli, then remove from the heat and set aside.

- Heat the vegetable oil in a large nonstick frying pan and cook the crab cakes for 2–3 minutes on each side, until hot and golden. Drain on kitchen paper and serve with lime wedges and the dipping sauce.

---

10 Crab and Rice Salad with Lime Dressing

Flake 2 x 175 g (6 oz) cans crab meat, and toss with 3 chopped spring onions, 1 deseeded and finely chopped red chilli, 3 tablespoons finely chopped coriander and the finely grated rind of ½ lime. Stir in 500 g (1 lb) cooked basmati rice, mix and spoon into bowls. Make the dipping sauce following the main recipe and serve warm, drizzled over the salad.

20 Crab Fried Rice

Lightly beat 2 small eggs with 1 tablespoon soy sauce and 1 teaspoon fish sauce. Heat 2 tablespoons oil in a frying pan and add half the egg, swirling to make a thin omelette. Cook for about 2 minutes, turning once, until slightly crispy. Remove from the pan and roll. Repeat to make another omelette roll. Return the pan to the heat with 2 tablespoons oil, and add 3 chopped spring onions, 1 deseeded and chopped red chilli and a 1.5-cm (¾-inch) piece of fresh root ginger, chopped. Cook for 2–3 minutes, until soft. Stir 500 g (1 lb) cooked basmati and wild rice mix into the pan, along with 100 g (3½ oz) defrosted frozen peas. Cook for 2–3 minutes, then add 2 x 175 g (6 oz) cans crab meat, flaked, and cook for a minute more, until hot. Spoon the fried rice into bowls, then slice the egg rolls thinly and scatter over the rice. Serve drizzled with extra soy sauce.

3⓪ Lemon Grilled Fish with Cheesy Mashed Potato

Serves 4

3 tablespoons chopped mixed
  herbs (such as chives, parsley,
  rosemary and oregano)
4 tablespoons olive oil
1 garlic clove, crushed
finely grated rind of 1 lemon
4 thick fish fillets, such as cod,
  haddock, pollack or coley, about
  150 g (5 oz) each
1 kg (2 lb) floury potatoes, peeled
  and cut into chunks
2 tablespoons lemon juice
50 g (2 oz) Parmesan-style
  cheese, grated
salt and pepper
steamed green beans, to serve

- Mix 1 tablespoon of the chopped herbs and 1 tablespoon of the oil with the garlic, lemon rind and a little seasoning, then massage over the fish fillets. Set aside for 10–15 minutes to marinate.

- Meanwhile, cook the potatoes in a large saucepan of lightly salted boiling water for 12–15 minutes, or until tender.

- Heat a ridged grill pan and cook the fish fillets, skin side down, for 4–5 minutes, until the skin is crispy. Turn the fish over, turn off the heat and set aside for 3–4 minutes until the fish is cooked. Keep warm.

- Drain the potatoes, return to the pan and place over a gentle heat for 1–2 minutes to dry them out. Add the lemon juice, cheese, remaining herbs and remaining olive oil. Season to taste and mash until smooth, then spoon on to 4 warmed plates. Serve the cheesy mash with the grilled fish and steamed green beans.

1⓪ Lemon, Prawn and Butter Bean Salad

Rinse and drain 2 x 400 g (13 oz) cans of butter beans and place in a bowl with 200 g (7 oz) cooked peeled prawns, 3 tablespoons chopped fresh mixed herbs, the rind and juice of 1 lemon, 2 tablespoons olive oil and plenty of seasoning. Toss gently to combine, then add 75 g (3 oz) rocket leaves. Heap on to 4 shallow dishes and serve garnished with lemon wedges and Parmesan shavings, if desired.

2⓪ Lemon-Mashed Butter Beans with Fish

Place 2 x 400 g (13 oz) cans drained and rinsed butter beans into a saucepan with 3 tablespoons chopped fresh mixed herbs, 1 crushed garlic clove, 2 tablespoons lemon juice, the finely grated rind of 1 lemon and seasoning. Add 100 ml (3½ fl oz) hot vegetable stock and simmer gently, covered, for 10–15 minutes, until the beans are really tender. Meanwhile, heat a large nonstick frying pan and rub 1 tablespoon oil over the fish fillets. Season generously and cook, skin side down, for 4–5 minutes, until the skin is crispy. Turn the fish over and cook the other side for 2–3 minutes, until just cooked. Mash the beans with 2 tablespoons oil and 50 g (2 oz) grated Parmesan-style cheese, then season to taste. Spoon on to 4 dishes and top with the fish, skin side up. Serve with steamed green beans, if desired.

Smoked Trout and Rice Noodle Salad

Serves 4

3 tablespoons vegetable or groundnut oil

1 teaspoon Thai fish sauce

1 tablespoon lime juice

1 tablespoon light soy sauce

375 g (12 oz) cold cooked rice noodles

200 g (7 oz) smoked trout trimmings, cut into strips

1 bunch of fresh coriander, chopped

1 red chilli, deseeded and chopped

1 small cucumber, finely sliced

1 red pepper, finely sliced

- Combine the oil, fish sauce, lime juice and soy sauce in a jar with a tight-fitting lid, and shake well to combine.

- Place the noodles in a large bowl with the remaining ingredients and toss with the dressing. Heap into 4 deep bowls and serve.

Hot and Sour Noodle Soup with Crispy Trout

Heat 1.2 litres (2 pints) stock in a saucepan with 3 tablespoons fish sauce, 1 tablespoon rice vinegar, 1 tablespoon lime juice and 1 tablespoon brown sugar. Add 1 deseeded and chopped red chilli, 1 tablespoon chopped fresh root ginger and 1 sliced garlic clove. Simmer for 12–15 minutes. Meanwhile, heat 1 tablespoon sesame oil in a frying pan and cook 4 trout fillets, about 125 g (4 oz) each, skin side down, for 7–8 minutes. Turn and cook for a further 1–2 minutes. Divide 375 g (12 oz) cold cooked rice noodles between 4 bowls and pour over the broth. Top each with a fish fillet and serve scattered with chopped coriander.

Marinated Salmon with Warm Noodle Salad

Place 4 salmon steaks, about 150 g (5 oz) each, in a shallow ovenproof dish. Mix 1 tablespoon honey in a bowl with 1 tablespoon dark soy sauce, 1 tablespoon lime juice, 1 teaspoon Thai fish sauce, 1 deseeded and finely chopped red chilli, 1 crushed garlic clove and 1 teaspoon finely grated fresh root ginger. Massage into the salmon and marinate for 12–15 minutes. Meanwhile, thickly slice 2 spring onions, cut 1 carrot into matchsticks and slice 1 red pepper. Place the salmon in a preheated oven, 200°C (400°F), Gas Mark 6, for 10–12 minutes, turning once, until just cooked. Remove and keep warm. Cook 200 g (7 oz) thick dried rice noodles in a pan of lightly salted boiling water for about 8 minutes, or according to packet instructions, until just tender. Heat 2 tablespoons oil in a large frying pan, add the prepared vegetables and cook for 3–4 minutes, until beginning to soften. Drain the noodles and toss with the vegetables, then heap into bowls and top with the salmon steaks and any juices. Serve scattered with chopped coriander.

BUD-FISH-DIW

Spaghetti with Broccoli, Lemon and Prawns

Serves 4

400 g (13 oz) spaghetti
2 tablespoons olive oil
½ teaspoon chilli flakes (optional)
200 g (7 oz) cooked peeled
  prawns
grated rind and juice of 1 lemon
1 small bunch of basil leaves,
  shredded
350 g (11½ oz) broccoli, cut into
  small florets
salt and pepper
handful of rocket leaves, to serve

- Cook the spaghetti in a large saucepan of lightly salted boiling water for 11 minutes, or according to packet instructions, until al dente.

- Meanwhile, heat the olive oil in a small pan and warm the chilli flakes for 1 minute, if using. Add the prawns, lemon rind and juice and basil leaves, season to taste and heat through.

- Cook the broccoli in a small saucepan of lightly salted boiling water for 2–3 minutes, until beginning to soften slightly. Drain and add to the prawns.

- Drain the pasta, return to the pan and add the prawn and broccoli mixture. Toss well to combine and heap into 4 shallow bowls. Serve topped with a few rocket leaves.

Broccoli, Lemon and Prawn Salad Blanch 350 g (11½ oz) broccoli florets in a small saucepan of lightly salted boiling water for 2–3 minutes, then cool under running water and drain. Make a dressing by combining 1 deseeded and finely chopped red chilli with 1 tablespoon lemon juice, 3 tablespoons oil, a pinch of grated lemon rind and a little salt and pepper. Whisk to combine. Toss 150 g (5 oz) rocket leaves with 200 g (7 oz) cooked peeled prawns, 1 small bunch of basil leaves, shredded, 2 finely sliced spring onions and the broccoli, and arrange on 4 plates. Drizzle over the dressing and serve.

Broccoli and Prawn Bake Cook 300 g (10 oz) farfalle pasta in a large saucepan of lightly salted boiling water for 11 minutes, or according to packet instructions, until al dente. Meanwhile, heat 50 g (2 oz) each of butter and flour in a saucepan with 575 ml (18 fl oz) milk, stirring constantly until thickened and smooth. Simmer for 1–2 minutes to cook the flour. Cook 350 g (11½ oz) broccoli florets in lightly salted boiling water for 2–3 minutes, until beginning to soften slightly, then drain and place in a large bowl with ½ teaspoon chilli flakes, 300 g (10 oz) cooked peeled prawns, 1 tablespoon lemon juice, and salt and pepper to taste. Stir 150 g (5 oz) crème fraîche into the white sauce and add to the bowl with the drained pasta. Stir gently to combine, then pour into a large, ovenproof dish. Sprinkle with 100 g (3½ oz) fresh breadcrumbs, then drizzle with 1 tablespoon oil and cook in a preheated oven, 200°C (400°F), Gas Mark 6, for 15–20 minutes until bubbling and lightly golden. Serve with rocket leaves.

 # Creamy Salmon and Spinach Filo Tarts

Serves 4

50 g (2 oz) butter, melted, plus extra for greasing

250 g (8 oz) frozen leaf spinach, defrosted

4 tablespoons double cream

150 g (5 oz) cream cheese

2 tablespoons chopped dill or chives

250 g (8 oz) salmon fillet, cut into 1-cm (½-inch) cubes

4 filo pastry sheets, approximately 45 x 25 cm (18 x 10 inches)

hollandaise sauce, to serve (optional)

salt and pepper

- Preheat the oven to 200°C (400°F), Gas Mark 6, and lightly grease a baking sheet. Place the spinach in the middle of a clean tea towel, bring up the edges and twist the spinach in the tea towel over a sink to squeeze out the excess moisture. Chop roughly, then place in a bowl with the double cream, cream cheese, herbs and seasoning. Mix well to combine, then gently fold in the diced salmon. Set aside.

- Brush both sides of the filo pastry sheets with the melted butter, then cut in half widthways to create 8 pieces, approximately 23 x 25 cm (9 x 10 inches). Place one half of each sheet over the other to form 4 crosses.

- Spoon the salmon mixture into the centre of each pastry cross and scrunch up the edges of the pastry towards the filling, without completely covering it, to make 4 tarts.

- Transfer the tarts to the baking sheet and cook in the preheated oven for 12–15 minutes, until the pastry is golden and the fish is just cooked. Remove and serve with a drizzle of warmed hollandaise sauce, if desired.

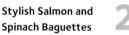

Stylish Salmon and Spinach Baguettes

Drain 2 x 175 g (6 oz) cans salmon and flake into a bowl. Add 4 tablespoons mayonnaise, 2 tablespoons chopped dill or chives, 2 teaspoons lemon juice and some black pepper. Mash with a fork until combined and spread over the bottom halves of 4 mini baguettes. Top with 125 g (4 oz) baby spinach leaves, then squeeze over extra lemon juice and season. Replace the lids and serve cut in half.

Creamy Salmon and Spinach Puffs

Unroll a 375 g (12 oz) sheet ready-rolled puff pastry and cut into quarters to make 4 rectangles. Brush with beaten egg and place on a greased baking sheet in a preheated oven, 220°C (425°F), Gas Mark 7, for 8–10 minutes until golden and puffed up. Meanwhile, melt 50 g (2 oz) butter in a large pan and add 400 g (13 oz) bite-sized chunks of boneless, skinless salmon fillet. Cook for 2–3 minutes, turning occasionally, until lightly golden. Stir in 150 g (5 oz) cream cheese, 150 ml (¼ pint) double cream, 250 g (8 oz) defrosted frozen leaf spinach and 2 tablespoons chopped dill or chives, then season with a little salt and plenty of freshly ground black pepper. Simmer gently for 4–5 minutes, until the salmon is cooked, divide between 4 warmed plates and top each portion with a piece of pastry. Serve with baby spinach leaves.

20 Spiced Mackerel and Couscous Salad

Serves 4

250 g (8 oz) couscous
3 tablespoons olive oil
2 teaspoons harissa
300 ml (½ pint) boiling water
  or vegetable stock
2 x 125 g (4 oz) cans mackerel
  fillets in brine, drained
½ red onion, finely sliced
1 small bunch of parsley,
  roughly chopped
150 g (5 oz) cherry tomatoes,
  halved
1 small cucumber, deseeded
  and diced
2 tablespoons lemon juice
16 black olives (optional)
salt and pepper

- Place the couscous in a bowl with ½ tablespoon of the olive oil, half the harissa and a little salt and pepper. Stir with a fork until well coated. Pour over the measured boiling water or vegetable stock, then cover and set aside for 5–8 minutes, until the grains are tender and the liquid has been absorbed. Uncover, fluff with a fork and tip into a large, shallow bowl to cool.

- Meanwhile, flake the mackerel and toss together with the red onion, parsley, cherry tomatoes and cucumber.

- Combine the remaining olive oil and harissa with the lemon juice. Season to taste and set aside.

- Fold the mackerel salad into the cooled couscous with half of the dressing, and spoon into 4 shallow bowls. Serve scattered with the olives, if using, and drizzled with extra dressing.

---

10 Cheat's Mackerel and Couscous Salad

Spoon 500 g (1 lb) ready-made couscous salad into 4 shallow bowls and flake 2 x 175 g (6 oz) cans mackerel fillets in spicy tomato sauce over the top. Scatter with 150 g (5 oz) halved cherry tomatoes and chopped parsley, and serve.

Harissa-Baked Mackerel with

Couscous Use a sharp knife to make 3 slashes in each side of 4 whole scaled and gutted mackerel. Mix 1 tablespoon harissa with 1 tablespoon lemon juice, 1 tablespoon olive oil and a little seasoning. Rub all over the mackerel and place in an ovenproof dish. Bake in a preheated oven, 200°C (400°F), Gas Mark 6, for 20–25 minutes until the fish is cooked. Meanwhile, place 250 g (8 oz) couscous in a bowl and stir in ½ tablespoon olive oil, 1 tablespoon harissa and a little salt and pepper. Pour over 300 ml

(½ pint) vegetable stock, cover and set aside for 5–8 minutes, until the grains are tender and the liquid has been absorbed. Uncover, fluff up with a fork and keep warm. Make a salad by combining ½ finely sliced red onion, 1 small bunch of parsley, roughly chopped, 150 g (5 oz) halved cherry tomatoes, 1 small deseeded and diced cucumber and 16 black olives. Drizzle with 1½ tablespoons olive oil and 1 tablespoon lemon juice. Serve the spicy baked mackerel with the steamed couscous and the prepared salad.

# Lemony Tuna and Borlotti Bean Salad

Serves 4

grated rind and juice of 1 lemon
3 tablespoons olive oil
2 spring onions, finely sliced
2 x 175 g (6 oz) cans tuna in oil or
spring water, drained and flaked
2 x 400 g (13 oz) cans borlotti
beans, drained and rinsed
1 small bunch of flat leaf parsley,
roughly chopped
75 g (3 oz) rocket or rocket
and watercress
salt and pepper

- Combine the lemon rind and juice and olive oil, and season with salt and pepper.

- Gently mix together all of the remaining ingredients and spoon into 4 shallow bowls. Drizzle with the dressing and serve immediately.

20 Seared Tuna with Warm Borlotti

Beans Heat 2 tablespoons olive oil in a frying pan and cook 1 chopped red onion for 7–8 minutes. Add 2 x 400 g (13 oz) cans borlotti beans, drained and rinsed, 1 bunch flat leaf parsley, chopped, and 125 ml (4 fl oz) vegetable stock. Season and simmer for 7–8 minutes. Rub 1 tablespoon oil over 4 small tuna steaks and season. Heat a griddle pan and cook the tuna for 3–4 minutes, turning once, until seared outside but pink inside. Set aside. Spoon the beans on to 4 warmed plates and top each with a seared steak. Garnish with a few rocket leaves and squeeze over the juice of 1 lemon to serve.

30 Griddled Tuna and Borlotti

Bean Niçoise Salad Rub 1 tablespoon oil over 2 tuna steaks, approximately 150 g (5 oz) each, then season generously. Heat a griddle pan and cook the tuna steaks for 4–5 minutes, turning once, until almost cooked through. Remove, place in a dish and set aside to cool for about 15 minutes. Boil 2 eggs in a small pan of water for 6 minutes, then cool under cold running water. Finely chop 1 green pepper and 1 small red onion, then deseed and dice 3 ripe but firm tomatoes. Place in a bowl with a 400 g (13 oz) can borlotti beans, drained and rinsed, 1 small bunch of flat leaf parsley, roughly chopped, and 75 g (3 oz) rocket leaves. Toss to combine, then divide between 4 plates. Shell the eggs and cut into wedges. Flake the tuna and arrange over the salads with the eggs. Drizzle with lemon juice and olive oil, and serve with crusty bread.

Nasi Goreng-Style Rice with Pilchards

Serves 4

250 g (8 oz) long-grain rice

500 ml (17 fl oz) boiling water

5 tablespoons vegetable oil, plus extra for greasing

3 eggs

1 large onion, chopped

2 garlic cloves, chopped

3 tablespoons nasi goreng paste or Thai chilli paste

½ Chinese cabbage or 1 small, green cabbage, shredded

2 tablespoons ketjap manis or sweet soy sauce

425 g (14 oz) can of pilchards or sardines in brine, drained and flaked

125 g (4 oz) cooked peeled prawns (optional)

salt and pepper

½ cucumber, diced, to serve (optional)

- Cook the rice in a large saucepan with the water according to packet instructions, until the rice is tender and the liquid has been absorbed. Fluff with a fork to separate the grains, then spread over a large, lightly oiled baking sheet to cool.

- Meanwhile, beat the eggs in a bowl and season well. Heat 2 tablespoons of the oil in a large nonstick frying pan and add half the beaten egg. Swirl the pan so that the egg covers the base thinly. Cook for 30–60 seconds, until almost set, then flip over and cook the other side for 30 seconds. Slide out of the pan and roll up tightly, then set aside to cool. Repeat with the remaining egg to make a second omelette.

- Heat the remaining oil in the pan, add the onion and garlic, and cook for 7–8 minutes, until soft and lightly golden. Stir in the nasi goreng or Thai chilli paste, and stir-fry for 1 minute. Stir in the shredded cabbage and cook gently for 3–4 minutes, until soft, then stir in the ketjap manis or sweet soy sauce and half of the pilchards or sardines, mashing them into the vegetables. Stir in the rice and heat through. Once the rice is hot, add the prawns, if using, and the remaining fish, folding gently to combine. Heat for a further 2–3 minutes.

- Meanwhile, slice the omelettes thinly and fold half of the shredded omelette into the rice. Spoon the rice into 4 shallow bowls, and top with the remaining sliced omelette and the diced cucumber, if using. Serve immediately.

Grilled Nasi Goreng Sardines Make 3 slashes in each side of 12–16 gutted and scaled sardines, and rub with 2 tablespoons nasi goreng or Thai chilli paste. Arrange on a foil-lined grill rack and cook under a preheated grill for 4–5 minutes, turning once. Meanwhile, heat 3 tablespoons oil with 1 more tablespoon paste, and add 3 sliced spring onions and ½ shredded Chinese cabbage. Cook for 4–5 minutes, until soft, then stir in 500 g (1 lb) ready-cooked basmati rice. Stir-fry for 2–3 minutes, then spoon on to 4 plates. Top each with 3–4 grilled sardines and serve garnished with ½ diced cucumber, if desired.

Nasi Goreng For this quicker version, use 500 g (1 lb) bought ready-cooked basmati rice. Follow the main recipe but omit the omelettes and instead fry 4 small eggs in a hot pan for 1–2 minutes, until slightly crispy. Serve one on top of each bowl of nasi goreng.

BUD-FISH-HYP

Crunchy-Topped Cod and Leek Pasta Bake

Serves 4

25 g (1 oz) butter
3 tablespoons olive oil
150 g (5 oz) streaky bacon, chopped
2 leeks, thinly sliced
350 g (11½ oz) quick-cook fusilli
500 g (1 lb) ripe tomatoes, diced
1 teaspoon finely grated lemon rind
2 tablespoons chopped herbs
  (such as parsley, chives, basil,
  rosemary or oregano)
375 g (12 oz) skinless chunky cod,
  coley or pollack fillet, cut into
  bite-sized pieces
2 tablespoons grated Parmesan-
  style cheese
75 g (3 oz) fresh breadcrumbs
salt and pepper

- Preheat the oven to 220°C (425°F), Gas Mark 7. Melt the butter in a large, deep-sided frying pan with 1 tablespoon of the oil, and cook the bacon for 2–3 minutes, stirring occasionally, until cooked and lightly golden. Add the leeks and cook for 2–3 minutes, stirring occasionally, until softened.

- Meanwhile, cook the pasta according to packet instructions.

- Add the tomatoes to the bacon and leeks along with half the lemon rind and half the herbs, then season and simmer for 2–3 minutes, until the tomatoes begin to soften. Stir in the chunks of cod, then cover and simmer gently for 2–3 minutes.

- Meanwhile, mix the Parmesan with the remaining lemon rind and herbs and the breadcrumbs, and season generously.

- Stir the drained pasta into the tomato sauce and transfer to a large ovenproof dish. Sprinkle over the breadcrumb mixture, drizzle with the remaining oil and bake in the preheated oven for 12–15 minutes, until the cod is cooked and the topping is crunchy.

10 Cod, Leek and Bacon Arrabbiata

Heat 2 tablespoons oil in a frying pan and cook 150 g (5 oz) chopped bacon for 4–5 minutes. Add 375 g (12 oz) skinless cod, cut into chunks, and a 350 g (11½ oz) jar arrabbiata pasta sauce. Bring to the boil, reduce the heat and simmer, covered, for 3–4 minutes. Heat 25 g (1 oz) butter in a saucepan and cook 2 sliced leeks for 6–7 minutes. Cook 350 g (11½ oz) quick-cook fusilli according to packet instructions. Drain and divide between 4 bowls. Stir the leeks into the sauce and serve over the pasta.

20 Bacon-Wrapped Cod with Leeks

Cook 350 g (11½ oz) penne pasta according to packet instructions, until al dente. Meanwhile, melt 25 g (1 oz) butter in a large, deep-sided frying pan with 1 tablespoon oil, and cook 2 thinly sliced leeks for 5–6 minutes, until soft and golden. Add 500 g (1 lb) diced ripe tomatoes to the leeks with ½ teaspoon finely grated lemon rind and 1 tablespoon chopped fresh mixed herbs, then season and simmer for 2–3 minutes, until the tomatoes begin to soften. Rub 1 tablespoon oil over 4 skinless, boneless cod fillets, then season and wrap each one in a rasher of rindless streaky bacon. Heat a nonstick frying pan and cook the wrapped cod for 6–8 minutes, turning once, until both the cod and the bacon are cooked and lightly golden. Serve the cod on a bed of pasta with the tomato sauce, sprinkled with another tablespoon of herbs.

Garlic Breaded Salmon with Spring Onion Mash

Serves 4

1 kg (2 lb) floury potatoes, peeled and cut into chunks

3 day-old white bread slices, crusts removed

1 teaspoon dried garlic powder

2 tablespoons chopped mixed herbs (such as parsley, chives and chervil)

1 egg, beaten

2 tablespoons seasoned flour

4 skinless, boneless salmon fillets, approximately 150 g (5 oz) each

3 tablespoons vegetable oil

50 g (2 oz) butter

75 ml (3 fl oz) single cream

4 spring onions, thinly sliced

salt and pepper

lemon wedges, to garnish

steamed broccoli, to serve

- Cook the potatoes in a large saucepan of lightly salted boiling water for 12–15 minutes, until tender.

- Meanwhile, place the bread in a mini-chopper or food processor with the garlic and herbs, blend to create fine breadcrumbs and tip on to a plate.

- Pour the beaten egg into a shallow bowl and the seasoned flour on to a plate. Coat the salmon fillets in flour, then dip each fillet in the egg and turn to coat. Roll in the plate of garlicky breadcrumbs until well coated.

- Heat the oil in a large nonstick frying pan and cook the breaded salmon fillets for 6–7 minutes, turning once, until crisp and golden on the outside but still a little pink in the middle. Drain on kitchen paper and keep warm.

- Drain the potatoes and return to the pan with the butter and cream. Season well and mash until smooth. Stir in the spring onions and spoon on to 4 warmed plates. Top each mound with a crispy breaded salmon fillet, garnish with lemon wedges and serve with steamed broccoli.

1 0 Pan-Fried Salmon with Spring Onion Mash Heat 3 tablespoons oil in a large frying pan and fry 4 skinless, boneless salmon fillets, about 150 g (5 oz) each, for 7–8 minutes, turning once. Meanwhile, heat 1 kg (2 lb) ready-made mashed potato and stir in 4 sliced spring onions. Blitz 100 g (3½ oz) ready-made garlic and herb croûtons in a mini-chopper or food processor. Serve the salmon fillets with the mashed potatoes, scattered with the crushed croûtons.

3 0 Healthy Garlic Salmon with Spring Onion Mash Follow the main recipe to coat 4 skinless, boneless salmon fillets in garlic breadcrumbs. Place on a lightly greased baking sheet and bake in a preheated oven, 190°C (375°F), Gas Mark 5, for 15–20 minutes until golden. Meanwhile, cook 1 kg (2 lb) floury potatoes, peeled and cut into chunks, in a large saucepan of lightly salted boiling water for 12–15 minutes, until tender. Drain the potatoes, return to the pan and pour in 100 ml (3½ fl oz) skimmed milk. Season well and mash until smooth, then stir in 4 thinly sliced spring onions. Serve with steamed broccoli and lemon wedges.

QuickCook

Something Sweet

Recipes listed by cooking time

30

20

10

 Chocolate and Nut Fondue

Serves 4

100 g (3½ oz) dark chocolate
100 g (3½ oz) milk chocolate
125 ml (4 fl oz) double cream
finely grated rind of 1 orange
3 tablespoons chopped
   mixed nuts

To serve

strawberries
shortbread fingers or other
   plain biscuits
marshmallows

- Place the chocolate, cream and orange rind in a heatproof bowl over a pan of barely simmering water, so that the bowl is not quite touching the surface of the water. Leave to melt very gently for about 10 minutes, then remove from the heat and stir until smooth.

- Meanwhile, toast the nuts in a small, dry pan over a medium-low heat for 2–3 minutes, stirring frequently, until golden brown. Tip on to a plate and leave to cool slightly for 2–3 minutes.

- Pour the melted chocolate into a small fondue pot or attractive serving bowl and scatter over the toasted nuts. Serve with a choice of strawberries, biscuits and marshmallows for dipping, with 4 long fondue forks or metal skewers to spear them on.

Chocolate Bar Fondue Place 175 g (6 oz) Toblerone, or similar Swiss chocolate with nougat or nuts, broken into chunks, in a small pan with 125 ml (4 fl oz) double cream and a few drops of orange extract. Warm over a very low heat for 7–8 minutes, stirring occasionally, until melted and smooth. Pour into a fondue pot or bowl and serve immediately, with fruit, biscuits and marshmallows, following the main recipe.

 Decadent Chocolate-Dipped Fruit and Nuts Melt 200 g (7 oz) dark chocolate in a heatproof bowl over a pan of barely simmering water, so that the bowl is not quite touching the surface of the water. Stir until smooth, and then dip a combination of whole nuts (such as walnuts, almonds, pecans and macadamias) and whole strawberries into the chocolate so that they are about two-thirds coated. Place on a baking sheet lined with baking paper and chill in the refrigerator for 15–20 minutes, until hardened. Serve with espresso coffee.

BUD-SWEE-FYH

 # Lime Cheesecake

Serves 4-6

200 g (7 oz) digestive biscuits, crushed
100 g (3½ oz) butter, melted
finely grated rind of 1 lime, plus 1½ tablespoons juice
300 g (10 oz) cream cheese
75 g (3 oz) icing sugar
slices of lime, halved, to decorate

- Tip the crushed biscuits into a bowl and stir in the melted butter until well coated. Line the sides of a loose-bottomed 20-cm (8-inch) cake tin with clingfilm, then replace the base and press the biscuit mixture evenly over the bottom of the tin. Chill in the refrigerator while making the filling.

- Meanwhile, place the lime rind and juice in a clean bowl with the cream cheese and icing sugar, and beat until smooth. Remove the base from the refrigerator, spoon over the filling and smooth down with a palette knife. Decorate with slices of lime. Return to the refrigerator for 20–25 minutes.

- Remove from the tin and gently peel away the clingfilm. Cut into slices and serve.

10 Upside-Down Cheesecake Mix together 200 g (7 oz) crushed digestive biscuits and 100 g (3½ oz) melted butter until well coated. Beat the finely grated rind of 1 lime and 1½ tablespoons lime juice in a bowl with 125 ml (4 fl oz) Greek yogurt, 150 g (5 oz) cream cheese and 75 g (3 oz) icing sugar until smooth. Spoon into 4 attractive glass serving dishes and serve sprinkled with the buttery digestive crumbs.

20 Lime Cheesecake Sandwiches
Place the finely grated rind of 1 lime and 1½ tablespoons lime juice in a bowl with 300 g (10 oz) cream cheese and 75 g (3 oz) icing sugar, and beat until smooth. Chill the cheesecake filling in the refrigerator for 15 minutes. Divide the mixture between 8 digestive biscuits, then top each one with a second biscuit. Serve immediately.

BUD-SWEE-JYD

Crunchy Baked Apples and Pears

Serves 4

400 g (13 oz) can apple slices
  in juice
400 g (13 oz) can pear quarters
  in juice
125 g (4 oz) apple compote
  or purée
50 g (2 oz) ground almonds
  or hazelnuts
50 g (2 oz) chopped mixed nuts
100 g (3½ oz) fresh breadcrumbs
50 g (2 oz) caster sugar
1 teaspoon ground cinnamon
  or mixed spice (optional)
50 g (2 oz) butter, melted
custard, to serve

- Preheat the oven to 200°C (400°F), Gas Mark 6. Mix the apples and pears with the compote and transfer to an ovenproof dish.

- Mix the ground and chopped nuts with the breadcrumbs, sugar and spices, if using. Mix in the melted butter until well coated, then spoon over the fruit. Bake in the preheated oven for 20–25 minutes, until crunchy and golden. Serve hot with warmed custard.

---

1 Apple and Pear Smoothie Drain a 400 g (13 oz) can apple slices in juice and a 400 g (13 oz) can pear quarters in juice, reserving the juice, and tip into a large jug blender with 1 roughly chopped banana, a pinch of ground cinnamon, 300 ml (½ pint) of the reserved juice and 125 ml (4 fl oz) Greek yogurt. Blend until smooth, then pour into 4 ice-filled glasses and serve immediately.

2 Crunchy-Topped Apple and Pear Purée Place 50 g (2 oz) ground almonds or hazelnuts in a large, dry frying pan with 25 g (1 oz) fresh breadcrumbs and 25 g (1 oz) caster sugar and 1 teaspoon ground cinnamon or mixed spice, if using. Toast gently, stirring constantly, for 8–10 minutes, until golden. Tip into a large, shallow bowl to cool. Meanwhile, drain a 400 g (13 oz) can apple slices in juice and a 400 g (13 oz) can pear quarters in juice, and blend in a food processor until smooth. Spoon into 4 individual glass serving dishes. Whip 150 ml (¼ pint) double cream until thick and spoon over the puréed fruit. Sprinkle over the crunchy topping and serve.

20 Sweet Almond Frittata

Serves 4

5 large eggs
125 g (4 oz) icing sugar
75 ml (3 fl oz) double cream
50 g (2 oz) ground almonds
1 teaspoon vanilla extract
  (optional)
25 g (1 oz) butter
50 g (2 oz) flaked almonds
vanilla ice cream or crème
  fraîche, to serve

- Beat the eggs in a large bowl with 100 g (3½ oz) of the icing sugar, the cream, ground almonds and vanilla extract, if using. Preheat the oven to 200°C (400°F), Gas Mark 6.

- Melt the butter in a large ovenproof frying pan and pour in the egg mixture. Cook very gently for 8–10 minutes, stirring occasionally, until the egg just begins to set. Scatter over the flaked almonds and sprinkle with the remaining icing sugar, then place in the preheated oven for about 10 minutes, until set.

- Remove the pan from the oven and cook under a preheated grill for 2–3 minutes, until golden, then cool slightly and cut into slices. Serve with vanilla ice cream or crème fraîche.

10 Sweet Almond Grilled Pancakes

Beat 50 g (2 oz) ground almonds, 1 teaspoon vanilla extract and all but 2 tablespoons of 125 g (4 oz) icing sugar into 200 g (7 oz) mascarpone. Divide the mixture between 8 small, ready-made sweet pancakes, then fold over and arrange in a large ovenproof dish. Scatter with 50 g (2 oz) flaked almonds and sprinkle over the reserved icing sugar. Cook under a preheated grill for 3–4 minutes, until warmed and lightly golden.

30 Sweet Almond Macaroons

Mix 125 g (4 oz) ground almonds with 50 g (2 oz) caster sugar. In a separate large bowl, beat 2 large egg whites with ½ teaspoon vanilla extract until stiff. Gently fold in the ground almond mixture until combined. Line 2 large baking sheets with baking paper and place teaspoonfuls of the mixture on the baking sheets, leaving room to spread. Bake in a preheated oven, 180°C (350°F), Gas Mark 4, for about 15 minutes until just firm. Remove from the oven, leave on the trays for 3–4 minutes, then transfer to a wire rack to cool.

 # Strawberry Yogurt Crunch

Serves 4

4 tablespoons strawberry jam

3 tablespoons dark soft brown sugar

500 ml (17 fl oz) Greek yogurt

8 digestive biscuits

1 small chocolate-covered honeycomb bar or extra digestives, crushed, to decorate

- Spoon the strawberry jam into the bottoms of 4 tall glasses. Stir the brown sugar into the Greek yogurt and divide half the mixture between the glasses.

- Place the digestive biscuits in a freezer bag and crush with a rolling pin, then use the crumbs to cover the yogurt. Spoon over the remaining yogurt and serve sprinkled with shards of chocolate-covered honeycomb or extra crushed digestives.

---

 2 Marinated Strawberry

Crunch Chop 250 g (8 oz) hulled strawberries and mix with 1 teaspoon lemon juice, 1 tablespoon brown sugar and the seeds from ½ vanilla pod. Cover and set aside for 15 minutes. Place 8 digestive biscuits in a freezer bag and crush with a rolling pin, then divide the crumbs between 4 glass serving bowls. Top with 500 ml (17 fl oz) Greek yogurt, spoon over the strawberries and serve immediately.

3 Strawberry Yogurt Crunch Muffins

Mix 100 g (3½ oz) melted butter in a jug with 125 ml (4 fl oz) strawberry yogurt, 2 lightly beaten eggs and 1 teaspoon finely grated lemon rind. In a large bowl, mix together 100 g (3½ oz) caster sugar, 150 g (5 oz) plain flour, 50 g (2 oz) chopped almonds, 1 teaspoon baking powder and ½ teaspoon bicarbonate of soda. Pour the wet mixture into the dry ingredients and mix gently until just combined. Use to fill a 12-hole muffin tin lined with paper cases, and sprinkle 1 extra tablespoon chopped almonds over the tops of the muffins. Bake in a preheated oven, 180°C (350°F), Gas Mark 4, for 18–20 minutes until risen and golden. Cool slightly on a wire rack, then serve warm with strawberry jam, if desired.

BUD-SWEE-TEY

 # Creamy Vanilla Rice Pudding

Serves 4

125 g (4 oz) pudding rice
about 750 ml (1¼ pints)
   whole milk
50 g (2 oz) caster sugar
1 teaspoon vanilla extract or
   1 vanilla pod, split
25 g (1 oz) butter

- Place all the ingredients in a saucepan and bring to the boil. Reduce the heat and simmer gently for 25–28 minutes, stirring frequently and adding more milk if necessary, until the rice is creamy and just tender.

- Remove the vanilla pod, if using, spoon the rice pudding into bowls and serve immediately.

---

1 **Crème Brûlée Rice Pudding** Spoon 600 g (1 lb 3½ oz) chilled ready-made rice pudding into 4 individual ovenproof dishes. Sprinkle the surface generously with 50 g (2 oz) caster sugar, then cook under a hot grill for 3–4 minutes, until the sugar begins to caramelize. Cool for a minute or two so that the sugar hardens, then serve immediately.

2 **Creamy Risotto-Style Rice Pudding** Melt 50 g (2 oz) butter in a saucepan, add 125 g (4 oz) pudding or risotto rice and cook, stirring, for 1 minute. Meanwhile heat 600 ml (1 pint) milk to simmering point, and stir in 50 g (2 oz) caster sugar and 1 teaspoon vanilla extract. Add the milk to the rice, a ladleful at a time, stirring constantly until all the milk has been absorbed and the rice is al dente. This should take 17–18 minutes. Spoon into bowls, sprinkle each one with a teaspoon of dark soft brown sugar and serve.

Banoffee Pancakes

Serves 4

4 large or 8 small ready-made sweet pancakes

6 tablespoons ready-made toffee sauce, warmed

2 bananas, sliced

150 ml (¼ pint) double or whipping cream

2 tablespoons coarsely grated dark chocolate or 2 chocolate digestive biscuits, crushed

- Place the pancakes on 4 plates and drizzle over the toffee sauce. Scatter the sliced bananas over half of each pancake, then fold over to enclose.

- Whip the cream to soft peaks, then place a spoonful on each pancake. Sprinkle with grated chocolate or crushed chocolate digestive biscuits and serve.

Baked Banoffee Split Place 4 large bananas on a baking sheet and cook in a preheated oven, 180°C (350°F), Gas Mark 4, for about 12 minutes until blackened and soft. Meanwhile, gently warm 6 tablespoons ready-made toffee sauce or 150 g (5 oz) dulce de leche in a small pan and whip 150 ml (¼ pint) double or whipping cream to soft peaks. Remove the baked bananas from the oven and cut a slit down the centre of each. Arrange in bowls and drizzle the warmed sauce over the bananas. Spoon over the whipped cream, sprinkle with the chocolate and serve.

Warm Banoffee Muffins Beat together 125 g (4 oz) each of softened butter, plain flour and caster sugar, 2 teaspoons baking powder and 2 eggs in a bowl. Mash 1 large, ripe banana and fold into the mixture. Use to fill a 12-hole muffin tin lined with paper cases and bake in a preheated oven, 180°C (350°F), Gas Mark 4, for about 20 minutes until risen and golden. Meanwhile, warm 6 tablespoons ready-made toffee sauce or 150 g (5 oz) dulce de leche in a small pan, and whip 150 ml (¼ pint) double or whipping cream to soft peaks.

Serve the warm muffins in a bowl, drizzled with the warm sauce and accompanied by a spoonful of whipped cream.

Melting Chocolate Pots

Serves 4

75 g (3 oz) dark chocolate
100 g (3½ oz) butter, plus extra
for greasing
75 g (3 oz) sugar
2 eggs
2 tablespoons cocoa powder
25 g (1 oz) plain flour
icing sugar, for dusting

- Preheat the oven to 180°C (350°F), Gas Mark 4, and butter 4 large ramekins, about 8 cm (3¼ inches) in diameter. Melt the chocolate and butter in a small pan over a very low heat.

- Meanwhile, beat the sugar and eggs together, and pour in the melted chocolate. Beat in the cocoa powder and flour, and continue beating until smooth.

- Divide the mixture between the ramekins and cook in the preheated oven for 10–12 minutes, or until crisp on top and still melting inside.

- Remove from the oven, set aside to cool for 1–2 minutes, then serve dusted with icing sugar.

Vanilla Ice Cream with Melting Chocolate Sauce Melt 175 g (6 oz) dark chocolate with 1 tablespoon golden or maple syrup, 15 g (½ oz) butter and 50 ml (2 fl oz) water in a heatproof bowl over a pan of barely simmering water, so that the bowl is not quite touching the surface of the water. Warm until melted, then mix until smooth and glossy. Serve drizzled over vanilla ice cream.

Dark Chocolate Soufflés Melt 125 g (4 oz) dark chocolate in a heatproof bowl over a pan of barely simmering water, so that the bowl is not quite touching the surface of the water. Heat gently until melted but not hot. Whisk in 3 egg yolks, then fold in 50 g (2 oz) self-raising flour. Whisk the 3 egg whites in a large bowl with 50 g (2 oz) caster sugar to form soft peaks. Gently fold the whisked egg whites into the chocolate. Lightly grease 4 individual ovenproof dishes or ramekins and place on a baking sheet. Divide the mixture between them and cook in a preheated oven, 190°C (375°F), Gas Mark 5, for 12–15 minutes until well risen. Serve immediately, dusted with icing sugar.

Sticky Toffee Apples

Serves 4

100 g (3½ oz) butter

1 tablespoon dark soft brown
sugar

1 teaspoon lemon juice

3 dessert apples, peeled, cored
and cut into 8 slices each

8 sheets of filo pastry, about
45 x 25 cm (18 x 10 inches)

For the toffee sauce

25 g (1 oz) butter

65 g (2½ oz) dark soft brown
sugar

50 ml (2 fl oz) double cream

- Preheat the oven to 180°C (350°F), Gas Mark 4, and line a baking sheet with baking paper. Melt half the butter in a frying pan with the sugar and lemon juice. Add the apples and cook for 8–10 minutes. Meanwhile, melt the remaining butter and brush over 4 sheets of filo pastry. Top each buttered side with a second sheet of pastry. Brush again with butter and fold each double layer in half lengthways to form 4 rectangles.

- Remove the apples from the pan, reserving the pan and its juices. Divide the apples between the sheets of pastry, arranging them at one end. Fold the other end of the pastry over the top to cover the apples. Turn in the edges and roll them over to create 4 parcels. Arrange on the baking sheet and cook in the preheated oven for 12–15 minutes.

- Meanwhile, make the toffee sauce by placing the butter, brown sugar and double cream in the frying pan. Stir over a low heat until the sugar has melted, then bubble for 1–2 minutes, until thick and deep golden. Remove from the heat to cool.

- Remove the apple parcels from the oven and serve drizzled with toffee sauce.

 Sticky Apple Skewers Melt 50 g (2 oz) butter in a pan with 50 ml (2 fl oz) double cream and 50 g (2 oz) dark soft brown sugar. Stir until the sugar dissolves, then simmer for 1 minute. Remove from the heat and set aside. Meanwhile, peel and core 4 dessert apples and cut into chunks. Toss in 1 teaspoon lemon juice. Thread the apple on to 8 small wooden skewers and arrange on serving plates. Add a scoop of vanilla ice cream to each plate and drizzle with toffee sauce.

Caramelized Apple Layer Peel, core and cut 3 dessert apples into about 1.5-cm (¾-inch) dice. Melt 50 g (2 oz) butter in a large frying pan with 1 tablespoon dark brown sugar and 1 teaspoon lemon juice. Add the apples and cook for 8–10 minutes, turning occasionally, until softened and golden. Remove from the heat and cool slightly. Meanwhile, crush 150 g (5 oz) ginger biscuits in a freezer bag with a rolling pin until they resemble fine breadcrumbs, and mix with 50 g (2 oz) melted butter to combine. Spoon the apples and biscuit crumbs into 4 serving glasses in layers, and top each one with a small scoop of ice cream or Greek yogurt and a sprinkle of sugar. Serve immediately.

 # Old-Fashioned Rock Cakes

Serves 4

250 g (8 oz) self-raising flour
1½ teaspoons baking powder
1 teaspoon mixed spice
125 g (4 oz) cold butter, diced
100 g (3½ oz) demerara or
  granulated sugar, plus extra
  for sprinkling
1 teaspoon grated orange rind
  (optional)
125 g (4 oz) mixed dried fruit
50 g (2 oz) mixed peel or
  chopped glacé cherries, or extra
  mixed dried fruit
1 large egg, beaten
3–4 tablespoons milk

- Preheat the oven to 180°C (350°F), Gas Mark 4, and line a baking sheet with baking paper. Place the flour, baking powder and mixed spice in a food processor with the butter and pulse until the mixture resembles fine breadcrumbs. Tip into a large bowl, then stir in the sugar, orange rind, if using, dried fruit and mixed peel.

- Pour in the beaten egg and add enough milk to bind the mixture to a soft, slightly sticky dough.

- Use 2 forks to make 8 rock-like mounds of the mixture on the prepared baking tray. Sprinkle with a little extra sugar and cook in the preheated oven for 18–20 minutes, until the rock cakes are golden and a skewer inserted into the middle comes out clean. Transfer to a wire rack to cool a little before serving.

 Rock Cake Yogurt Place 125 g (4 oz) mixed dried fruit and 50 g (2 oz) mixed peel or chopped glacé cherries in a small pan with 1 teaspoon grated orange rind, 50 ml (2 fl oz) orange juice, ½ teaspoon mixed spice and 2 tablespoons light soft brown sugar. Warm gently, stirring occasionally, until the sugar has dissolved. Set aside to cool slightly, then spoon the fruit mixture into 4 individual glass dishes. Top each dish with 100 ml (3½ fl oz) Greek yogurt, then crumble over a soft amaretti biscuit or shortbread biscuit to serve.

Banana, Raisin and Cinnamon Mini Rock Cakes Sift 250 g (8 oz) self-raising flour with 1½ teaspoons baking powder and ½ teaspoon ground cinnamon. Rub in 125 g (4 oz) diced cold butter until the mixture resembles fine breadcrumbs, then stir in 1 small mashed banana and 50 g (2 oz) raisins. Bind with 1 large beaten egg and a little milk, if necessary, then arrange 16–20 small spoonfuls of the mixture on a large baking sheet lined with baking paper. Cook in a preheated oven, 190°C (375°F), Gas Mark 5, for 8–10 minutes until cooked and golden, then transfer to a wire rack to cool.

30 Spiced Shortbread Squares with Toffee Ice Cream

Serves 4

150 g (5 oz) butter
75 g (3 oz) caster sugar, plus
  extra for rolling
200 g (7 oz) plain flour
½–1 teaspoon ground cinnamon
  or mixed spice
4 scoops of toffee ice cream

- Preheat the oven to 180°C (350°F), Gas Mark 4, and line a baking sheet with baking paper.

- Place the butter and sugar in a food processor and blend until well mixed. Add the flour and spice, and blend to just combine. Tip out on to a smooth surface and knead lightly to form a soft dough.

- Shape into a 15-cm (6-inch) long, square-sided cylinder and roll in the extra sugar. Flatten the sides slightly, to give the dough a square cross-section. Cut into approximately 16 square slices and place on the prepared baking sheet. Cook in the preheated oven for about 15 minutes, until lightly golden.

- Transfer to a wire rack to cool slightly, then serve warm with scoops of toffee ice cream.

1 Millionaire's Shortbread

Ice Cream Crumble 125 g (4 oz) shortbread fingers into 4 individual glass serving dishes. Top each with a scoop of vanilla ice cream and drizzle with a tablespoon of warmed toffee sauce or dulce de leche. Sprinkle each serving with 1 tablespoon chocolate chips and serve immediately.

2 Chocolate-Covered

Shortbread Melt 200 g (7 oz) orange-flavoured dark chocolate in a heatproof bowl over a pan of barely simmering water, so that the bowl is not quite touching the surface of the water. Open a packet of 12 shortbread fingers and dip half of each biscuit in the melted chocolate. Arrange on a baking sheet lined with baking paper and chill in the refrigerator for 10–15 minutes. Serve with scoops of chocolate ice cream.

30 Ginger and Treacle Sponge

Serves 4

175 g (6 oz) golden syrup
125 g (4 oz) soft butter
  or margarine, plus extra
  for greasing
125 g (4 oz) caster sugar
2 eggs
125 g (4 oz) self-raising flour
1½ teaspoons ground ginger
single cream or custard,
  to serve

- Preheat the oven to 180°C (350°F), Gas Mark 4, and grease an ovenproof dish. Pour the golden syrup into the bottom of the dish.

- Place all of the remaining ingredients in a bowl and beat until smooth, then pour it over the golden syrup. Smooth with a spatula to make an even layer, then cook in the preheated oven for 20–25 minutes, until risen and golden.

- Serve drizzled with cream or warmed custard.

10 Quick Ginger and Treacle-Drizzled Sponge

Place 1 tablespoon black treacle in a small pan with 50 g (2 oz) butter, 75 g (3 oz) light soft brown sugar, 1½ teaspoons ground ginger and 100 ml (3½ fl oz) double cream. Heat until the sugar has dissolved and the mixture is smooth and glossy. Arrange 4 slices of warmed Madeira cake on 4 serving plates, then drizzle with the ginger and treacle sauce and serve with cream or custard.

20 Ginger Syrup Biscuits

Beat 125 g (4 oz) softened butter in a bowl with 1 egg, 1½ teaspoons ground ginger, 3 tablespoons golden syrup and 50 g (2 oz) caster or demerara sugar. Add 175 g (6 oz) self-raising flour and mix to combine. Place spoonfuls of the mixture on a large baking sheet lined with baking paper, leaving room to spread, and bake in a preheated oven, 180°C (350°F), Gas Mark 4, for about 10 minutes until golden. Cool on a wire rack and serve.

Quick Cherry Tiramisu

Serves 4

6 tablespoons icing sugar, sifted

100 ml (3½ fl oz) strong black coffee

12 sponge fingers

200 g (7 oz) mascarpone or cream cheese

150 ml (¼ pint) double cream

2 tablespoons crème de cassis or syrup from canned cherries

425 g (14 oz) can black cherries in light syrup, drained

- Stir 2 tablespoons of the icing sugar into the coffee. Arrange the sponge fingers in the bottoms of 4 individual glass dishes, then pour over the black coffee and set aside to soak for about 5 minutes.

- Meanwhile, beat the remaining icing sugar into the mascarpone and double cream with the crème de cassis or cherry syrup. Spoon over the sponge fingers and chill in the refrigerator for 10–15 minutes. Spoon the drained cherries on top to serve.

Cheat's Cherry Tiramisu
Divide 400 g (13 oz) can of cherry pie filling between 4 individual glass serving dishes. Beat the cream with 300 ml (½ pint) Greek yogurt and 1 tablespoon honey, until thickened, then crumble 6 sponge fingers into the mixture. Spoon on to the cherries and serve dusted with cocoa powder.

Golden Baked Cherries and Pears
Drain and chop a 400 g (13 oz) can pear halves in juice, and tip into an ovenproof dish with 425 g (14 oz) can black cherries, drained. Place 75 g (3 oz) butter in a food processor with 200 g (7 oz) self-raising flour and pulse until the mixture resembles fine breadcrumbs. Add 50 g (2 oz) caster sugar and 150 ml (¼ pint) Greek yogurt, then pulse to just combine. Spoon over the cherries and pears, and cook in a preheated oven, 200°C (400°F), Gas Mark 6, for 20–25 minutes until golden. Serve with warmed custard.

BUD-SWEE-ZAE

 # Carrot Cake Scones with Cream Cheese

Serves 4

200 g (7 oz) self-raising flour
½ teaspoon ground cinnamon
½ teaspoon ground nutmeg
pinch of salt
50 g (2 oz) butter, plus extra
  for greasing
25 g (1 oz) caster sugar
50 g (2 oz) carrot, peeled and
  finely grated
50 g (2 oz) raisins
1 teaspoon finely grated
  orange rind
2–3 tablespoons milk,
  plus extra for brushing

For the cream cheese filling

150 g (5 oz) cream cheese
3 tablespoons icing sugar, sifted
1 teaspoon vanilla extract
  (optional)

- Preheat the oven to 220°C (425°F), Gas Mark 7, and lightly grease a baking sheet. Mix the flour in a bowl with the ground spices and salt. Rub in the butter until the mixture resembles fine breadcrumbs, then stir in the sugar. Stir in the grated carrot, raisins and orange rind, then add enough milk to make a soft dough.

- Knead very lightly on a lightly floured surface, then pat flat to a thickness of 1.5 cm (¾ inch). Cut into about 8 triangles, using up any remaining dough to make more scones. Place on the prepared baking sheet and brush with a little milk. Cook in the preheated oven for about 12 minutes, until risen and golden.

- Meanwhile, make the filling. Beat the cream cheese in a bowl with the icing sugar and vanilla extract, if using, until smooth. Set aside.

- Remove the scones from the oven and cool slightly on a wire rack. Split the warm scones in half, spread cream cheese on one half, then reassemble and serve.

---

1 Fruit Scones with Cream Cheese

Warm 4–8 ready-made fruit scones in a preheated oven, 180°C (350°F), Gas Mark 4, for 3–4 minutes, or according to packet instructions. Meanwhile, beat 150 g (5 oz) cream cheese in a bowl with 3 tablespoons sifted icing sugar and 1 teaspoon vanilla extract, if using, until smooth. Serve the cream cheese filling with the warm scones.

2 Quick Carrot Cake Scones

Place 325 g (11 oz) ready-made plain scone mix in a large bowl, add 50 g (2 oz) raisins, 50 g (2 oz) grated carrot, ½ teaspoon ground cinnamon and ½ teaspoon ground nutmeg, and mix according to packet instructions to make a dough, adding an extra splash of milk if necessary. Knead very lightly on a lightly floured surface, then pat flat to a thickness of 1.5 cm (¾ inch) and cut into about 8 triangles. Place the scones on a lightly greased baking sheet and bake in an oven preheated to 220°C (425°F), Gas Mark 7 until golden and cooked. Split and butter the scones while still warm.

Lemon Tart with Vanilla Cream

Serves 4

200 g (7 oz) lemon curd

1 sweet pastry tart case, about
23 cm (9 inches) across

250 g (8 oz) strawberries, hulled
and sliced

1 vanilla pod, split lengthways

200 ml (7 fl oz) double cream

1 tablespoon icing sugar

- Spread the lemon curd over the base of the tart case, then scatter over the sliced strawberries.

- Scrape the seeds from the vanilla pod into the cream with the icing sugar and whip until it forms soft peaks. Spoon over the strawberries and serve immediately.

Lemony Vanilla Fool Divide 100 g (3½ oz) lemon curd between 4 individual glass serving dishes. In a large bowl, beat 200 ml (7 fl oz) Greek yogurt with 200 g (7 oz) mascarpone, the seeds from 1 vanilla pod and 100 g (3½ oz) more lemon curd. In a separate bowl, whip 200 ml (7 fl oz) double cream until it forms soft peaks, then fold gently into the lemony mascarpone. Spoon the mixture into the glasses and chill for 10 minutes before serving with crisp biscuits.

Lemon and Vanilla Mousse Place 200 ml (7 fl oz) double cream, the seeds from 1 vanilla pod, grated rind of 1 lemon and 50 g (2 oz) sugar in a large bowl, and whip until it forms soft peaks. Whisk 2 egg whites in a clean bowl until stiff and fold gently into the cream with 3 tablespoons lemon curd. Spoon another 150 g (5 oz) lemon curd into 4 tall serving glasses, then top with the mousse. Chill in the refrigerator for 15–20 minutes, or until ready to serve.

BUD-SWEE-NEK

 # Pear and Walnut Muffins

Serves 4

250 g (8 oz) plain flour
100 g (3½ oz) dark soft brown
  sugar
1 teaspoon baking powder
¾ teaspoon bicarbonate of soda
½ teaspoon ground cinnamon
50 g (2 oz) walnut pieces,
  chopped
250 ml (8 fl oz) plain yogurt
50 g (2 oz) butter, melted
2 large eggs, beaten
2 canned pear halves in juice,
  diced
2 tablespoons honey, warmed,
  to serve (optional)

- Preheat the oven to 180°C (350°F), Gas Mark 4. Mix the dry ingredients together in a large bowl. Whisk the remaining ingredients together in another bowl. Now pour the wet ingredients into the dry and stir with a large spoon until just combined.

- Use the mixture to fill a 12-hole muffin tin lined with paper cases and bake in the preheated oven for 15–18 minutes, until risen and golden. Cool a little on a wire rack, then serve drizzled with warmed honey, if desired.

---

1   Warm Honeyed Pears with Walnuts

Place 50 g (2 oz) butter, 2 tablespoons honey and ½ teaspoon ground cinnamon in pan, and warm gently until melted and smooth. Drain 2 x 400 g (13 oz) cans pear halves in juice, then slice thickly and arrange in shallow bowls. Pour over the warmed buttery honey and serve scattered with the walnut pieces.

2   Cinnamon-Baked Pears with Walnuts

Gently warm 50 g (2 oz) butter, 2 tablespoons honey and ½ teaspoon ground cinnamon in a pan until melted and smooth. Meanwhile, peel, halve and core 4 ripe but firm pears and place, cut sides down, in a snug-fitting ovenproof dish. Scatter with 50 g (2 oz) chopped walnuts, drizzle with the warm sauce and bake in a preheated oven, 190°C (375°F), Gas Mark 5, for 15 minutes until warmed through and slightly softened. Serve with bought muffins, if desired.

 # Ginger and Lemon Cupcakes

Serves 4

100 ml (3½ fl oz) groundnut
  or vegetable oil
125 ml (4 fl oz) natural yogurt
2 eggs, lightly beaten
1 teaspoon finely grated
  lemon rind, plus extra
  to decorate
100 g (3½ oz) caster sugar
150 g (5 oz) plain flour
1 teaspoon ground ginger
1 teaspoon baking powder
½ teaspoon bicarbonate of soda
icing sugar, to decorate

- Preheat the oven to 180°C (350°F), Gas Mark 4. Place all the ingredients in a large bowl and beat well until smooth.

- Use the mixture to fill a 12-hole muffin tin lined with paper cases and bake in the preheated oven for 15–18 minutes, until risen and golden. Cool on a wire rack and serve warm or cold, decorated with a sprinkling of icing sugar and finely grated lemon rind.

 ### Ginger and Lemon Cheesecakes

Crush 100 g (3½ oz) ginger biscuits in a freezer bag with a rolling pin and mix the crumbs with 2 tablespoons melted butter until well coated, then divide between 4 individual glass ramekins, pushing down with the back of a spoon to cover the bases. Beat together 1 teaspoon finely grated lemon rind, 150 ml (¼ pint) Greek yogurt, 150 g (5 oz) cream cheese or mascarpone and 1–2 tablespoons honey, according to taste. Spoon into the ramekins and serve immediately.

Ginger and Lemon Fruit Gratin

Drain 2 x 400 g (13 oz) cans apricots or peaches in juice and arrange in an ovenproof dish. In a bowl, beat together 350 ml (12 fl oz) Greek yogurt, 1 teaspoon finely grated lemon rind, 1 teaspoon ground ginger and 2 tablespoons dark soft brown sugar. Spoon over the fruit and smooth the surface. Sprinkle over a further 2 tablespoons dark soft brown sugar and cook under a preheated moderate grill for 7–8 minutes, until the sugar has melted and is beginning to caramelize. Cool slightly, then spoon into bowls to serve.

Buttery Brioche Pudding

Serves 4

50 g (2 oz) butter, softened, plus extra for greasing
8 thick slices of brioche
3 eggs, beaten
4 tablespoons sugar
450 ml (¾ pint) whole milk
1 teaspoon vanilla extract (optional)
75 g (3 oz) sultanas
single cream, to serve (optional)

- Preheat the oven to 180 °C (350 °F), Gas Mark 4, and grease a large ovenproof dish. Spread butter over both sides of each brioche slice. Heat a nonstick frying pan and fry the brioche slices for 1–2 minutes on each side, until crisp and golden.

- Whisk together the eggs, sugar, milk and vanilla extract, if using.

- Arrange the brioche slices in the prepared ovenproof dish, scatter with sultanas and pour over the egg mixture. Cook in a preheated oven for 20–25 minutes, until just set and lightly golden. Serve with single cream for pouring, if desired.

---

1 Buttery Brioche with Ice Cream

Spread both sides of 8 thick brioche slices with softened butter, then sprinkle with 4 tablespoons sugar. Heat a nonstick frying pan and fry the brioche slices for 1–2 minutes on each side, until crisp and golden. Cut into triangles and arrange on serving plates with scoops of vanilla ice cream and scattered with 75 g (3 oz) sultanas.

2 Golden Brioche with Homemade Custard

Pour 600 ml (1 pint) whole milk into a saucepan with 1 teaspoon vanilla extract and heat to boiling point, then remove from the heat. Meanwhile, whisk 4 egg yolks in a large bowl with 25 g (1 oz) caster sugar and 2 teaspoons cornflour. Whisk the hot milk into the eggs, then return the mixture to the pan and warm over a very low heat, stirring constantly, until thickened, taking care not to boil. Remove from the heat and keep warm. Meanwhile, toast 8 slices of brioche in butter and sugar following the 10-minute recipe. Cut into triangles, arrange in bowls scattered with sultanas and serve drizzled with warm custard.

BUD-SWEE-FAM

 # Fallen Fruit Crumble

Serves 4

2 dessert apples, peeled, cored and cut into wedges

2 pears, peeled, cored and cut into wedges

200 g (7 oz) fresh or frozen blackberries

2 tablespoons orange juice

100 g (3½ oz) light soft brown sugar

75 g (3 oz) butter, softened

125 g (4 oz) plain flour

3 tablespoons oats

1 teaspoon ground mixed spice

2 tablespoons honey

250 ml (8 fl oz) Greek yogurt

- Preheat the oven to 200°C (400°F), Gas Mark 6. Place the fruit in a large saucepan with the orange juice and one-quarter of the sugar, and warm over a medium heat for 4–5 minutes, stirring occasionally, until the fruit begins to soften.

- Meanwhile, rub the butter into the flour until the mixture resembles fine breadcrumbs, and stir in the remaining sugar, the oats and half the mixed spice.

- Tip the fruit into an ovenproof dish and sprinkle over the crumble topping. Cook in the preheated oven for about 20 minutes, until golden.

- While the crumble is in the oven, stir the honey and remaining mixed spice into the yogurt, and chill until required. Serve the crumble hot with the spiced yogurt.

 Fallen Fruit Granola Peel and core 2 dessert apples and 2 pears. Cut into wedges and place in a large saucepan with 200 g (7 oz) fresh or frozen blackberries, 2 tablespoons orange juice and 100 g (3½ oz) light soft brown sugar. Warm over a medium heat for 4–5 minutes, stirring occasionally. Once the fruit has softened slightly, spoon into dishes and top each one with 50 g (2 oz) ready-made crunchy oat granola. Serve with the spiced yogurt, as above.

 Forest Fruit Crunch Place 500 g (1 lb) frozen mixed fruits in a saucepan with 50 g (2 oz) sugar and 1 teaspoon finely grated orange rind. Warm until the fruit has defrosted and the sugar dissolved, then pour into an ovenproof dish. Meanwhile, crush 200 g (7 oz) sweet oat biscuits in a freezer bag with a rolling pin and mix with 1 teaspoon ground mixed spice and 25 g (1 oz) flaked almonds, if desired. Sprinkle the topping over the fruit and cook in a preheated oven, 200°C (400°F), Gas Mark 6, for about 10 minutes until hot and golden. Serve dusted with icing sugar, with spoonfuls of the spiced yogurt, as above.

10 Almond Affogato

Serves 4

4 scoops of nougat or vanilla
   ice cream
4 drops of almond extract
4 shots of hot strong coffee
1 tablespoon flaked almonds,
   toasted
almond biscuits, to serve
   (optional)

- Place a scoop of ice cream into each of 4 heatproof serving glasses. Stir the almond extract into the hot coffee, then pour 1 shot over each scoop of ice cream. Scatter with the toasted almonds and serve with almond biscuits, if desired.

20 Affogato-Inspired Cookies

Beat 150 g (5 oz) softened butter and 250 g (8 oz) sugar together until pale and creamy, then beat in 1 teaspoon coffee extract and 1 egg. Add 250 g (8 oz) plain flour, ½ teaspoon bicarbonate of soda and 100 g (3½ oz) chopped almonds, and mix to combine. Arrange 16–20 small spoonfuls of the mixture on 2 large, lightly greased baking sheets, leaving room to spread. Cook in a preheated oven, 180°C (350°F), Gas Mark 4, for 6–8 minutes until lightly golden. Transfer to wire racks to harden and cool slightly. Serve with ice cream and strong espresso coffee.

30 Affogato-Style Tiramisu

Stir 4 drops of almond extract into 125 ml (4 fl oz) cold strong coffee. Arrange 16 sponge fingers in a dish, then pour over the coffee and set aside for 5 minutes to soak. Break up the sponge fingers and divide half of them between 4 tall freezer-proof glasses. Spoon a small scoop of nougat or vanilla ice cream into each of the glasses, and top with the remaining sponge fingers. Top with another small scoop of ice cream, then place in the freezer for 10–15 minutes, until firm. Sprinkle with a dusting of cocoa powder and 1 tablespoon toasted flaked almonds and serve with almond biscuits or rolled ice-cream wafers, if desired.

Raspberry Ripple Pain Perdu

Serves 4

325 g (11 oz) frozen raspberries
1 teaspoon lemon juice
2 tablespoons icing sugar, plus
extra for dusting
2 eggs, lightly beaten
125 g (4 oz) caster sugar
1 teaspoon vanilla extract
(optional)
250 ml (8 fl oz) whole milk
4 thick slices of day-old
farmhouse bread or brioche
75 g (3 oz) butter
crème fraîche, to serve (optional)

- Place the raspberries in a saucepan with the lemon juice and icing sugar, and warm very gently until just beginning to collapse. Blend in a food processor until smooth then pass through a sieve to remove the seeds.

- Whisk together the eggs, caster sugar and the vanilla extract, if using. Add the milk slowly, whisking until smooth and incorporated.

- Dip the slices of bread in the egg mixture, so that both sides are well coated. Melt the butter in a large nonstick frying pan and cook the egg-coated bread slices gently for about 2 minutes on each side, until crisp and golden.

- Remove the bread from the pan and arrange on serving plates. Drizzle with the warm raspberry coulis to create a ripple effect, then dust with icing sugar and serve immediately with crème fraîche, if desired.

Pain Perdu with Raspberry Ripple Ice Cream

Follow the main recipe to coat 4 thick slices of day-old farmhouse bread or brioche in the egg mixture, and fry the bread slices until golden. Remove from the pan and sprinkle both sides of the bread with demerara sugar. Arrange on serving plates and top each slice with a scoop of raspberry ripple ice cream and a dusting of icing sugar.

Baked Raspberry Pain Perdu

Cut 4 thick slices of day-old farmhouse bread or brioche into cubes and arrange in an ovenproof dish. Whisk 2 eggs with 1 extra egg yolk, 125 g (4 oz) caster sugar, 1 teaspoon vanilla extract and 250 ml (8 fl oz) whole milk, and pour over the cubes of bread. Scatter with 125 g (4 oz) fresh raspberries, and cook in a preheated oven, 180°C (350°F), Gas Mark 4, for about 20 minutes until just set and golden. Serve dusted with icing sugar, with crème fraîche, if desired.

 # Almost Instant Peach Trifle

Serves 4

175 g (6 oz) raspberry Swiss roll, sliced

400 g (13 oz) can sliced peaches in juice, drained, juice reserved

200 g (7 oz) mascarpone

200 g (7 oz) ready-made custard

2 tablespoons icing sugar

150 ml (¼ pint) double cream, whipped

25 g (1 oz) chocolate, grated, to decorate

- Use the Swiss roll slices to line the base of an attractive glass serving dish. Drizzle over 100 ml (3½ fl oz) of the reserved juice, then scatter over the sliced peaches.

- Beat the mascarpone with the custard and icing sugar, and spoon it over the fruit.

- Spoon the whipped cream over the custard, and decorate with the grated chocolate.

---

2 Orange Flower Poached Peaches

Cut 6 ripe but firm peaches or nectarines in half and remove the stones. Place in a saucepan with 500 ml (17 fl oz) water, 200 ml (7 fl oz) orange juice, 1 teaspoon orange flower water and 2 tablespoons icing sugar. Bring to the boil, then reduce the heat and simmer gently for 8–10 minutes, until tender. Pour into a large, shallow bowl and set aside to cool. Meanwhile, beat 2 teaspoons orange flower water into the mascarpone with 2 extra tablespoons icing sugar. Spoon the poached peaches into 4 bowls with as much of the cooking liquid as desired. Serve with the sweetened mascarpone and 8 sponge fingers.

---

3 Baked Peaches with Mascarpone

Cut 6 ripe but firm peaches or nectarines in half and remove the stones. Place the peaches, cut sides up, in a snug-fitting ovenproof dish. Mix 125 ml (4 fl oz) orange juice with 2 tablespoons honey and pour over the peaches. Sprinkle over 2 tablespoons icing sugar and cook in a preheated oven, 180°C (350°F), Gas Mark 4, for 15–18 minutes until tender. Meanwhile, beat 2 extra tablespoons icing sugar into the mascarpone and chill until required. Remove the peaches from the oven and arrange in serving dishes. Scatter over 100 g (3½ oz) fresh raspberries, if desired, and serve with the sweetened mascarpone.

BUD-SWEE-SEH

Giant Orange and White Chocolate Chip Cookies

Serves 4

150 g (5 oz) soft butter
  or margarine, plus extra
  for greasing
250 g (8 oz) caster sugar
finely grated rind of 1 orange or
  1 teaspoon orange essence
1 egg
250 g (8 oz) plain flour
pinch of salt
½ teaspoon bicarbonate of soda
150 g (5 oz) white chocolate,
  cut into chunks

- Preheat the oven to 180°C (350°F), Gas Mark 4, and lightly grease 2 nonstick baking sheets. Beat the softened butter and sugar together until pale and creamy, then beat in the orange rind or essence and the egg. Sift the flour, salt and bicarbonate of soda into the bowl, and mix to combine. Stir in the chocolate chunks.

- Arrange 6 large spoonfuls of dough on each of the 2 prepared baking sheets, leaving plenty of room for the dough to spread. Cook in the preheated oven for 10–12 minutes, until lightly golden.

- Transfer to wire racks to harden and cool slightly. Serve warm or cold. Any leftover cookies can be stored in an airtight tin for 2–3 days.

1 **White Chocolate and Orange Hot Chocolate** Coarsely grate 200 g (7 oz) white chocolate and place in a heatproof bowl. Heat 750 ml (1¼ pints) milk in a saucepan with 1 teaspoon orange essence until it just reaches boiling point, then pour it over the grated chocolate. Stir until completely melted, then divide between 4 mugs. Top each serving with a spoonful of whipped cream and extra white chocolate curls, if desired, and serve with ready-made white chocolate cookies.

3 **White Chocolate Blondies** Melt 375 g (12 oz) white chocolate and 75 g (3 oz) butter in a small saucepan over a very gentle heat and set aside. Meanwhile, break 3 eggs into a bowl with 125 g (4 oz) caster sugar, 1 teaspoon orange essence and the finely grated rind of 1 orange, and beat with a wooden spoon. Stir in the melted chocolate and 150 g (5 oz) self-raising flour, then pour into a lined and greased brownie tin, about 23 cm (9 inches) square. Cook in a preheated oven, 180°C (350°F), Gas Mark 4, for about 20 minutes, until golden and slightly risen but not too firm. Cool slightly, then cut into squares and serve warm with white chocolate or vanilla ice cream.

Index

Page references in *italics*
indicate photographs.

Acknowledgements

Executive editor: **Eleanor Maxfield**
Senior editor: **Leanne Bryan**
Copy-editor: **Jo Smith**
Art director: **Jonathan Christie**
Design: **Tracy Killick**
Art direction: **Juliette Norsworthy & Tracy Killick**
Photographer: **Bill Reavell**
Home economist: **Denise Smart**
Stylist: **Isabel De Cordova**
Senior production controller: **Caroline Alberti**